I0616386

Understanding
the Apostolic

Understanding the Apostolic

Dr. Noel Woodroffe

CONGRESS PUBLISHING HOUSE
LONDON ▪ JOHANNESBURG ▪ MIAMI ▪ PORT OF SPAIN

First Published in Trinidad & Tobago 2019 by
Congress Publishing House

Websites: http://www.elijahcentre.org
             http://www.congresswbn.org/

Copyright © 2019 Congress Publishing House
ISBN 978-976-43-0165-3
ISBN 978-1-7331153-0-8

All Rights Reserved
No part of this publication may be reproduced, stored in a retrieval system, or transmitted in any form or by any means, electronic, mechanical, photocopying, recording, or otherwise, without the prior written permission of the Publishers.

Quotations designated (NKJV) are from
The New King James Version (NKJV).
Copyright © 1982, Thomas Nelson, Inc. All rights reserved

Quotations designated (NIV) are from
The Holy Bible: New International Version® (NIV®)
Copyright © 1973, 1978, 1984, 2011 by International Bible Society www.ibs.org. All rights reserved worldwide. "

C O N T E N T S

O N E

T H E C A L L I N G O F

A N A P O S T L E

*T*he most powerful move of God since the birthing of the Church on the streets of ancient Jerusalem is sweeping across the nations of the earth, engulfing the Church in a fresh new mantle of power, purpose and deliberate strategic activity. The End is now definitely in sight, no longer just a concept at the outer limits of our faith. But it is now an attainable and reachable goal to this mighty generation in the earth today. This great move of God is called the **Apostolic Reformation.***

In every move of God there is an activating truth. Luther's move in the middle of the 16th century was activated by the restoration of the truth of justification by faith and the priesthood of all believers. The Pentecostal Move of God birthed in the USA at the start of the 20th century was signified by the activation of the baptism of the Holy Spirit and speaking

---

* Read my book: **The Present Reformation of the Church**.
Ordering details at the back of this volume.

in other tongues. The Apostolic Reformation is activated by the restoration and general acceptance in the Church of apostolic ministry once again in the Body of Christ.

Apostles have always been in the Church. Paul in Ephesians 4 says:

> [11] *And He Himself gave some to be apostles, some prophets, some evangelists, and some pastors and teachers,*
> [12] *for the equipping of the saints for the work of ministry, for the edifying of the body of Christ*
> [13] *till we all come to the unity of the faith and of the knowledge of the Son of God, to a perfect man, to the measure of the stature of the fullness of Christ;*
>
> **Ephesians 4: 11 – 13 NKJ**

They may have been mis-named, unrecognized and unaccepted, but the authority of Jesus Christ as head over His own Church has always caused them to be functional within the unfolding purposes of the Lord in the earth. Now there is a new recognition and acceptance, and the central figure of the apostle is bringing a 'new' technology to the Church.

Apostolic Qualifications

There are many false principles and definitions of apostolic ministry, and in these days of the amplification of the power of the gift, many are assuming the role and the title of apostle without the slightest comprehension of the nature and operation of the calling in God.

You are not an apostle because you:

Plant many churches	Peter did not plant many churches.
Possess great revelation	Barnabas wrote no books of revelatory truth.
Are senior in years in ministry	The original 12 apostles were quite young men.
Are leader of a ministry team	Barnabas was always second to Paul.
Travel a lot	James the apostle was permanently placed in Jerusalem.
Are prominent and popular	All the early apostles were persecuted and unpopular and nothing is known of the ministry of Matthias who replaced Judas.

These characteristics may operate to varying degrees of power in the ministry of an apostle but they do not constitute the basis upon which the recognition of the calling is made. Let us look at some verses in which Paul identifies significant features of the identity of the call of an apostle in his life.

Paul, called to be an apostle of Jesus Christ through the will of God...

1 Corinthians 1:1

Paul, an apostle (not from men nor through man, but through Jesus Christ and God the Father who raised Him from the dead),…

Galatians 1:1

Paul, an apostle of Jesus Christ, by the commandment of God our Savior and the Lord Jesus Christ, our hope,…

1 Timothy 1:1

…for which I was appointed a preacher and an apostle-- I am speaking the truth in Christ and not lying-- a teacher of the Gentiles in faith and truth.

1 Timothy 2:7

An apostle is called by the will of God. This is not a matter of human preference or of management technique or skill. The will of God is a mighty and powerful thing. It is not simply a divine preference; it has momentum, authority and spiritual force to it that cancels the opposition of all other powers in the earth. This power lies behind the calling of an apostle and gives the gifting an extraordinary amount of motivation to go forward to the fulfillment of the purposes of God here on earth.

You cannot become an apostle because you grew into the anointing and gifting. One does not enter into the function because of ordination by another person to be an apostle. It is not achieved by certification or by a course of study. The calling and the ordination come from above.

Apostles are Sent

The word 'apostle' is a transliteration of the Greek word *'apostolos'* which means *a sent one*. This is a very important dimension of the apostolic calling. To be sent one must have:

- Command/Purpose
- Movement/Momentum
- Direction/Vision
- Destination/Finish.

These important factors operate both in the natural and the spiritual dimensions of a sending.

Command or Purpose
Any activity that commences without a command originating from a source outside of the individual life and from a higher level of authority, cannot be described as a 'sending'. **To be sent, one must be activated by a command.** The impulse to move does not originate within the confines of our own life – the command comes from outside. The apostle obeys an exterior command and he is bound by it in obedience. The desire of the apostle to obey is part of the structure of the calling from God.

Paul endured beatings, persecutions and abuses in many places. In Derbe he was stoned by Jews who came from Antioch, dragged out of the city and left for dead *(Acts 14: 19 – 20)*. He later revived and went right back into the city to continue the work there. What motivated Paul? Did this desire to continue come from within his own will and determination?

No! He was a man under command, bound to obey that which was delivered to him from a higher authority.

When a General of the army commands a junior officer, that command explodes in the life of the soldier with urgent force. He becomes a 'sent' one who is released only when the command has been fulfilled. The command rearranges his priorities. He does not go home to dinner leaving the command of the General to be executed later. Every other command from authorities of lesser rank than the General become ineffective, and can only reassert their priority when he has fulfilled the command of the most senior officer of the army. Such it is with the apostolic function. He is sent by God to fulfill purpose and the very nature of the gifting is infused with these values.

Movement and Momentum

It is impossible to speak of a sending without realizing that the very definition of the word involves movement. Paralysis, passivity and stasis are actually enemies of a sending. Concepts of journeying and migration with purpose are essential to the understanding of a sent one. Thus the apostolic function is filled with movement, flexibility and the spirit of migration. The accurate spirit of the apostolic always calls the Church to journey to another place. The sending makes the current location obsolete. No one is sent to the place they are currently at – movement is always implied.

The force of the command that initiates the sending gives the movement the characteristic of momentum. Momentum is the mass/weight that lies behind the movement. It is a very different experience being run over by a baby's stroller traveling at five kilometers an hour, from being flattened by a cement mixer traveling at the same speed of five kilometers per hour. The speed of the movement is the same but the momentum behind the cement mixer flattens everything in its path.

The apostolic gifting is filled with momentum because of the mass or the weight of God that lies behind the motivational power of the sending. The apostolic is not apologetic and uncertain. It surges into confidence in the plan of God and does not give ground to the resistances of the enemy. It is filled with boldness, power to move forward and the awesome weight of the divine command.

Direction and Vision
I have already spoken of the fact that the apostolic mentality is filled with the spirit of migration or journeying. It is clear that the journey also involves the pursuit of a definite direction. **Movement without direction is not a journey; it has become wandering.** When God removed access to the land of Canaan from the tribes of Israel their journey immediately degenerated into wandering filled with daily death.

Accuracy can only be maintained in movement if a clear direction is taken and maintained. The principle behind a straight line is the principle of the continuous maintenance of consistent direction. All of this is part of the apostolic technology.

In the realm of the Spirit, accuracy of movement is maintained through the clear and consistent prophetic vision. In the Old

Testament, God maintained the forward movement of His patriarchs toward the eventual conclusion of their purposes in the earth, by the continuous provision of vision through His speaking and visions of the Lord. Time and time again He appeared to Abraham and on each occasion He provided more and more vision to clearly outline the way forward for the father of faith.

Vision is Certainty. The more vision we have the more we speak out of sure faith and certainty of the eventual outcome. This produces boldness of utterance, authority of action, strength of spiritual posture and a commitment to accuracy that is significant of developed apostolic positions.

Destination and Finish
The 'sent one' cannot be sent to nowhere. The attainment of a destination is critical to the reality of a sending. Both the end and the beginning are bound up in one. It is impossible to release the command that activates a sending without at the same time describing the end of the journey. Thus the 'sent one' is indescribably filled with destination-realization at the beginning of the journey.

Two characteristics occur in the apostolic gifting, the technology of the 'sent one':

Firstly: The sight of destination at the beginning of the journey provides the apostolic gifting with a great deal of focus and unswerving commitment to finishing the purposes of the Lord. Finishing becomes very important to the apostle. Every process is impregnated with the desire to finish the purposes of the

Lord. The apostolic thus is very committed, very focused and very single-minded to pursue the purposes of the Lord.

Secondly: The focus on the finish and the push to complete the journey and to fulfill the purpose of the sending refines the quality of the journey. It is not likely that the apostle will easily be diverted into cul-de-sacs, irrelevance and frivolity in ministry, purposeless religious activity, self-centered ambitious activity or any kind of function that will destroy the movement towards the finish. This is how Paul described his journey:
I have fought the good fight, I have finished the race, I have kept the faith.

2 Timothy 4: 7 NKJ

The finishing of the race involves the fighting of a good fight. The achievement of the finish depends on the refinement and the quality of the process along the way. Performance orientation, strong desire to please God, recognition of the power of the sending and the ferocious desire to finish and complete purpose are all part of the apostolic mentality. Jesus said:
... *"My food is to do the will of Him who sent Me, and to finish His work."*

John 4: 34 NKJ

In this declared mentality of Christ is found the core of the apostolic structure. God's will is only declared successful in the earth when proclamation is taken to execution. *Faith without works is dead!* The work must be taken to the finish and that statement includes all of the warfare, the expressed character, the endurance and fruit of the Holy Spirit that is required to complete against all the oppositions of both the satanic enemy and the carnal nature of man. This grandeur of spirit is essential to the apostolic function.

The Apostle and the Church

Ephesians 4: 11 - 13 NKJ
And He Himself gave some to be apostles, some prophets, some evangelists, and some pastors and teachers, for the equipping of the saints for the work of ministry, for the edifying of the body of Christ, till we all come to the unity of the faith and of the knowledge of the Son of God, to a perfect man, to the measure of the stature of the fullness of Christ;

All the five governmental ministry gifts were given by Christ to the Church for its edification or building up, but we speak in particular of the apostolic ministry. The apostolic ministry equips the saints. It is not given to build personal ministry empires. The apostle is one of God's tools to get the divine resource to where God really intends it to get to, which is, among the saints.

The word "equip" also means *to shape according to an already accepted standard.* The true standard is Christ Himself and the work of the apostolic is to transform and shape the saints into the standard of Christ. The apostolic does not come to bless only. The apostle never seeks to facilitate the self-indulgent desires of the believer to use God only for what is personally beneficial or comfortable. The aim of the apostle is to produce the Christ-standard in the lives and mentalities of the believers through the functioning of his ministry. The saints have to be brought to a place of effective work. The aim of the apostolic is the production of Kingdom purpose in the Body of Christ.

Thus we can say that God is more concerned about the distribution and impartation of the *'apostolic spirit'* on the Body than He is in exalting and promoting an individual apostolic gift. The purpose of the apostle is to release an apostolic spirit upon the corporate Church so that each individual believer can operate from an apostolic perspective and in an apostolic mentality.

To look at the nature of the individual apostolic anointing is to look at the nature of the corporate deposit that the apostle releases to the Church. God not only wants to raise up apostles but also apostolic saints and apostolic churches. He desires Kingdom Communities in which the rich deposit of each of the five governmental ministries is released into the hearts and lives of the saints, until they receive all of the fullness of Christ ordained for that particular Kingdom Community.

We can see this principle operating in the ministry of Jesus Christ. In *Luke Chapter 9* Jesus calls the twelve disciples to Him and commissions them for the first time to go out as apostles. He gives them very specific commands which constitute the mandate of their sending:

> ¹ *Then <u>He called His twelve disciples</u> together and gave them power and authority over all demons, and to cure diseases.*
> ² *He sent them to preach the kingdom of God and to heal the sick.*

³ And He said to them, "Take nothing for the journey, neither staffs nor bag nor bread nor money; and do not have two tunics apiece.
⁴ "Whatever house you enter, stay there, and from there depart.
⁵ "And whoever will not receive you, when you go out of that city, shake off the very dust from your feet as a testimony against them."
⁶ So they departed and went through the towns, preaching the gospel and healing everywhere.

Luke 9: 1 – 6 NKJ

And *the apostles, when they had returned*, told Him all that they had done. Then He took them and went aside privately into a deserted place belonging to the city called Bethsaida.

Luke 9: 10 NKJ

It is very evident that a transformational impartation has been released to them. It is not by chance that they are called the "disciples" in verse 1 and then called the "apostles" in verse 10. The agent of this impartation are the words of Jesus detailing the conditions of their apostolic activity, the characteristics of their operations and the release of the power to proclaim the Kingdom of God and to heal the sick. Thus we can see His words as the spiritual template for the transmission of the apostolic spirit and function into their lives. The new apostles return to declare the completion of the task and to give a report of all that they had done.

In *Luke Chapter 10* another interesting sending takes place:

> ¹ *After these things the Lord appointed seventy others also, and sent them two by two before His face into every city and place where He Himself was about to go.*
>
> ² *Then He said to them, "The harvest truly is great, but the laborers are few; therefore pray the Lord of the harvest to send out laborers into His harvest.*
>
> ³ *"Go your way; behold, I send you out as lambs among wolves.*
>
> ⁴ *"Carry neither money bag, knapsack, nor sandals; and greet no one along the road.*
>
> ⁵ *"But whatever house you enter, first say, 'Peace to this house.'*
>
> ⁶ *"And if a son of peace is there, your peace will rest on it; if not, it will return to you.*
>
> ⁷ *"And remain in the same house, eating and drinking such things as they give, for the laborer is worthy of his wages. Do not go from house to house.*
>
> ⁸ *"Whatever city you enter, and they receive you, eat such things as are set before you.*
>
> ⁹ *"And heal the sick there, and say to them, 'The kingdom of God has come near to you.'…"*

> **Luke 10: 1 – 9 NKJ**

This sending is different from the first. The number seventy is important and significant in the Word of God:

Deut. 10:22 / Gen. 46: 47	Jacob went into Egypt with 70 souls (The seed of the complete nation to come).

Numbers 11	Seventy elders are imparted to with the spirit of Moses in order to serve the entire body of Israel.
Judges 8:30	Gideon had 70 sons as a sign of the completion of his life's work.
Matthew 18:22	Jesus stipulates forgiveness 70 times seven as representing the complete work of grace in forgiving.

Seventy is the number that is representative of wholeness or completeness of community, action or spiritual state. It represents a condition that is significant of the entire Body. It is important to see that Jesus sent out the seventy in to "every city and place" where He was about to visit. The seventy represent the completeness of the ministry or the visitation of Christ in the entirety of His will. Thus the seventy that are sent out represent the fullness or the completeness of the Body of Christ, the Church.

The mandate given by Jesus to the seventy is the same as the mandate given to the twelve and yet the seventy are not apostles. The seventy go out under the same apostolic spirit, receiving from the same source the twelve received from, and to their complete shock and surprise they experience in their own lives the same power, the same results and similar demonstrations of authority as was seen in the experience of the twelve. They come back to Jesus in joy and triumph:

17 Then the seventy returned with joy, saying, "Lord, even the demons are subject to us in Your name."

18 And He said to them, "I saw Satan fall like lightning from heaven.

19 "Behold, I give you the authority to trample on serpents and scorpions, and over all the power of the enemy, and nothing shall by any means hurt you.

Luke 10: 17 - 19 NKJ

These represent the fullness of the Church operating under the authority of an apostolic spirit and producing Kingdom activity that is representative of the apostolic function. Verse 21 says: *"In that hour Jesus rejoiced in the Spirit..."* It was the prophetic hour of the Church being birthed into a new dimension of apostolic revelation, grace and authority. He does not "rejoice" at the return of the twelve but he does at the return of the seventy.

Though the book is called the Acts of the Apostles yet in it we see not only apostles in productive and powerful Kingdom activity, but we observe a completely activated and functional Church. Evangelists are taking cities, husband and wife teams are ministering openly; saints are fleeing Jerusalem and starting churches all over Europe and Asia Minor. There is confrontation of the political, literary, religious and economic systems of the day. Every aspect of the Church of the day is in the fullest force and expression of kingdom life. Such it is when the apostles are 'active' in the bosom of the Church.

The greatest contribution of the apostles rising in the Church today is the urgent release of an enabling, uplifting, empowering apostolic spirit to the entire Church in the earth, causing the Church to rise up in victory, purpose, power and strategic execution of the prophetic purposes of the Lord in the earth and bringing them to total and ultimate finish.

The Power of Apostolic Grace

Romans 1: 5 - 6 NKJ
Through Him we have received grace and apostleship for obedience to the faith among all nations for His name, among whom you also are the called of Jesus Christ;

The potent resource that flows from the apostolic position is called 'apostolic grace'. It is a significant and usable divine resource that can bring vast changes into the lives of those who receive. Let us look at several verses that deal with apostolic grace:

1 Corinthians 3: 10
<u>According to the grace of God which was given to me</u>, as a wise master builder I have laid the foundation, and another builds on it. But let each one take heed how he builds on it.

Galatians 2: 9
... and when James, Cephas, and John, who seemed to be pillars, <u>perceived the grace that had been given to me</u>, they gave me and Barnabas the right hand of fellowship, that we should go to the Gentiles and they to the circumcised.

Ephesians 3: 2-3
*if indeed you have heard of **the dispensation of the grace of***
***God which was given to me for you**, how that by*
revelation He made known to me the mystery (as I have briefly
written already …

Acts 4: 33
*And with **great power** the apostles gave witness to the*
*resurrection of the Lord Jesus. And **great grace** was upon*
them all.

The urgent divine resource which Paul received which he called "grace" was the defining factor of his apostolic gifting. It was the grace received that made him a wise master-builder and certified him to lay foundation in the emerging church in the earth at that time. That grace was so evident that it could be perceived by the senior apostles at Jerusalem in the lives of Barnabas and Paul, so much so that they gave to them the right hand of fellowship. But more important, the grace was given to Paul so that it could be distributed or transferred to the corporate entity of the Church – the grace was *"given to me for you…"*

The divine direction is always a movement from the individual to the corporate. He calls a single apostle that he might establish an apostolic company. God sets the solitary in families *(Psalm 68:6)*; he looks for a man to stand before him that he might bless an entire land *(Ezekiel 22:30)*. When the apostles minister in the city of Jerusalem with great power under the mighty impact of apostolic grace, it flows upon all the people and the Word records that "great grace" was upon them ALL. This is the preferred position of God – that great grace might be activated by powerfully called apostolic ministry but would flow upon all who would receive it.

The Reality of Apostolic Impartation

Impartation *is the direct transfer of grace or divine resource from God's realm of the Spirit to the earthly realm of man.* The word as it is used in the Word of God contains the concept of sharing and so when the apostle imparts, he shares his life, his anointing, his effective apostolic grace with those to whom he ministers.

In *Philippians Chapter 4* the church ministers to Paul with financial offerings and gifts to take care of his immediate needs and he in turn releases access to the dimension of God's grace that he represents:

> *18 Indeed I have all and abound. I am full, having received from Epaphroditus the things sent from you, a sweet-smelling aroma, an acceptable sacrifice, well-pleasing to God.*
>
> *19 And <u>my God shall supply all your need</u> according to His riches in glory by Christ Jesus.*
>
> **Philippians 4: 18 – 19 NKJ**

But perhaps the most significant scripture dealing with the matter of apostolic impartation is found in Paul's letter to the church in Rome:

> *9 For God is my witness, whom I serve with my spirit in the gospel of His Son, that without ceasing I make mention of you always in my prayers,*
>
> *10 making request if, by some means, now at last I may find a way in the will of God to come to you.*

> [11] *For I long to see you, that I may impart to you some spiritual gift, so that you may be established –*
> [12] *that is, that I may be encouraged together with you by the mutual faith both of you and me.*
> [13] *Now I do not want you to be unaware, brethren, that I often planned to come to you (but was hindered until now), that I might have some fruit among you also, just as among the other Gentiles.*
>
> **Romans 1: 9 – 13 NKJ**

The church in Rome is a mighty church whose faith was spoken of throughout the then known world *(verse 8)*. Strong churches, ministries and saints are not exempt from the need for an impartation of apostolic grace. Several factors are mentioned here that surround the release of an apostolic impartation.

Factors Surrounding Apostolic Impartation

Firstly: Apostolic impartation flows from accurate operations in the will of God. Paul wants to come to Rome to minister to the saints there, but he seeks to find a way in the will of God to come to them. Divine resources in the apostolic do not function correctly outside of correct discernment of the divine will.

The apostolic impartation does not come out of the resident gifts and graces activated by the Holy Spirit in our spirits – it is not a charismatic spiritual gift. It is part of the headship gift of Christ Himself to His own Church. We have already said that the apostle is a 'sent one'. The value of his function is that it lines up with the command and the desire of God Himself, therefore the accurate apostolic impartation always operates in agreement with the revealed will of God. Thus Paul strives to discern the accurate season allowed by God for his visit to the church in the city of Rome in order for an accurate impartation to occur.

Secondly: Paul indicates that the impartation released to the church at Rome will cause the church to be "established" (*verse 11*). The word is derived from a Greek word that means '*a prop*' and it indicates a process of stabilizing an object until it is perpendicular and not in danger of falling sideways.

When that concept is applied to a local community of believers under the power of the impartation from an apostolic gift, we can see immediately the beneficial impact of such an impartation. The apostolic impartation not only strengthens the foundations of a corporate community but also provides it with such a confirmation and affirmation in its spiritual development and growth and releases spiritual certainty.

I have seen this happen in ministries and churches in our global apostolic network. Cultures, languages or ethnic differences do not affect it. The apostolic impartation goes directly to the root of the spiritual structure regardless of any earthly conditions, and works the same in every culture. Wherever people of God receive the apostle, the apostolic impartation and the apostolic authority, there is an awesome impartation of the divine grace that builds, stabilizes and confirms the ministry in the things of God.

Thirdly: Paul indicates that there is a dimension of warfare and resistance that opposes the release of the apostolic impartation.

Paul has often planned to visit Rome and he does not want the saints there to be unaware of that fact. He has been prevented or hindered from making the trip to see them. Our position is that the prevention came from the satanic realm that did not want to see the church at Rome receive the strengthening that the apostolic visit would activate. To be fair I will say at this point that there are others who interpret this as indicating that Paul was prevented by God from coming until it was accurate and allowable in His will and that is a reasonable position also.

In any case the physical presence of the apostle among the saints in this strong Roman church would release divine dimensions from the spirit realm that were locked up until the apostle presented himself. His visit would change their position, their strength and their level of confirmation. Paul himself was not too certain of exactly what would occur, and was not sure of the nature of the spiritual changes that would follow his visit. He would discover that at the time of impartation, as the will of God released what the church would need at that hour for their confirmation. He was sure however that *"some spiritual gift"* would be released from the realm of the spirit to the waiting church.

The First-ness and Last-ness of Apostolic Ministry

1 Corinthians 12: 28 NKJ
And God has appointed these in the church: <u>first apostles</u>, second prophets, third teachers, after that miracles, then gifts of healings, helps, administrations, varieties of tongues.

Apostles are set or appointed by God in the church first. The word "first" is *'proton': first in time, rank or influence.*

This first-ness cannot be interpreted to mean superiority in quality over all the other ministries. Such a concept is not acceptable in a true perspective of the Kingdom of God.

All five governmental ministries are diverse expressions of the 'Christ' - the anointing without measure or limit. Paul indicated in *Ephesians 4:13* that the five gifts will continue to impart until *"we come to the measure of the stature of the fullness of Christ".* No part of Christ is superior or inferior to any other part. It is theologically impossible that there be different levels of perfectness in a being that is essentially divinely perfect as God is.

The first-ness of the apostolic has to do with its pioneering dimension and its breakthrough power. Such qualities are basic to the apostolic gift. I call it the **Bulldozer Dimension** of the apostolic. When God wishes to release new dimensions of doctrine, new positions of the Church, fresh advance of global Kingdom positions He does so by releasing apostles to accomplish the work.

But the apostles are also called "last" in the Church:
> *9 For I think that God has displayed us, the apostles, last, as men condemned to death; for we have been made a spectacle to the world, both to angels and to men.*
> *10 We are fools for Christ's sake, but you are wise in Christ! We are weak, but you are strong! You are distinguished, but we are dishonored!*

¹¹ To the present hour we both hunger and thirst, and we are poorly clothed, and beaten, and homeless.
¹² And we labor, working with our own hands. Being reviled, we bless;
¹³ being persecuted, we endure; being defamed, we entreat. We have been made as the filth of the world, the offscouring of all things until now.

1 Corinthians 4: 9 - 13 NKJ

The apostolic can survive under severe persecution and prosper in conditions that would discourage other dimensions of ministry. Martin Luther called himself a Catholic monk but he was an apostle of the Lord called to pioneer new positions for the Church in the earth. God's apostles are the first to sacrifice their lives for the Body but placed last under the feet of all men so that all can advance forward into the depths of God's purpose through their suffering and the price they pay in the earth. God's apostles are truly a resource to be utilized by all. Paul said it well in his letter to the Corinthians:

⁷ But we have this treasure in earthen vessels, that the excellence of the power may be of God and not of us.
⁸ We are hard pressed on every side, yet not crushed; we are perplexed, but not in despair;
⁹ persecuted, but not forsaken; struck down, but not destroyed –
¹⁰ always carrying about in the body the dying of the Lord Jesus, that the life of Jesus also may be manifested in our body.
¹¹ For we who live are always delivered to death for Jesus' sake, that the life of Jesus also may be manifested in our mortal flesh.
¹² So then death is working in us, but life in you.

2 Corinthians 4: 7 - 12 NKJ

As God causes the Church to move in this day to more exact and accurate positions in the Spirit, the entire structure of leadership in the Body of Christ is being adjusted. The leadership of the Church is not about titles, clerical robes, crosses hanging from necks, and hierarchical struggles for power and position. There is a Davidic reality that is emerging across the nations of the earth as God's true leadership from every culture, language and ethnic group are moved by the Spirit to the forefront of the true global Church.

The tribes of the true Church are coming to the covenant place of Hebron once again and with desiring for an accurate Spirit-led leadership to enable them to enter the depths of the prophetic purposes of the Lord. The people came to David at Hebron and said to him:

> *"Also, in time past, when Saul was king over us, you were the one who led Israel out and brought them in; and the LORD said to you, 'You shall shepherd My people Israel, and be ruler over Israel.'"*

> *2 Samuel 5: 2 NKJ*

There is a 'Saul' leadership that claims pre-eminence and yet has no power to lead the people in and out. Such favor and power are given to those who are truly of the structure and order of God – the Davidic order of leadership coming forth in the Apostolic Reformation and the formation of the 'new' Church.

The apostles that are being raised up by the Lord all across the earth in every nation are those who are being empowered by the Spirit to lead the Church past the foolishness, the entertainment, the politics, the materialism of the Babylonian invasions of the House of God to the places of actual and accurate entry into His divine purposes.

This is the cry of the Holy Spirit that is being heard in every quarter of the global Church. This is a season of hope for those whose hearts are truly seeking God. The apostolic anointing has returned with full power and accuracy to the earth and the Spirit of God is speaking through apostles once again in the released principles of the Kingdom all across the earth. Let us hear them!

TWO

TRUE AND FALSE
APOSTLES

*I*t is evident that if there is the release of accurate, genuinely called apostles in the Church in the midst of the current Apostolic Reformation move of God that there will also be the release of the counterfeit ministry of "false apostles". It is absolutely important that we acquaint ourselves with the principles from the Word that would allow us to identify clearly what is false in the realm of the apostolic, both for the purpose of rejecting that which does not line up with the principles of the word of God, and also so that we do not allow invasions of the false principles into our accurate ministries as we go further to build for God's Kingdom.

There is extensive discussion of false apostles by Paul in 2 *Corinthians Chapter 11*. Let us examine some of the issues concerning false apostles that Paul dealt with in this chapter.

False Apostles: Issues Dealt with by Paul

> ² *For I am jealous for you with godly jealousy. For I have betrothed you to one husband, that I may present you as a chaste virgin to Christ.*
> ³ *But I fear, lest somehow, as the serpent deceived Eve by his craftiness, so your minds may be corrupted from the simplicity that is in Christ.*
>
> **2 Corinthians 11: 2 – 3 NKJ**

Accurate apostolic ministry, Paul says, causes a betrothal of the heart of the people to Christ. His use of the prophetic picture of the chaste virgin indicates that the foundation of true apostolic ministry is purity and covenant. The apostle jealously guards the quality of the input into the saints and the local church. All aspects of spiritual adultery and harlotry are rejected by the accuracy of the apostolic.

Craftiness and Deception
The core principle of the false ministry is deception. As Paul indicates the serpent deceived Eve through "craftiness" and the principles used by the enemy in that encounter are the same strategies used by him today. Craftiness is: *'panourgia': the exercise of false or empty wisdom.* It describes that which seems to be true but really has no substance. Therefore, false apostles cause enslavement of the mind through deceptive teaching that seems to be accurate, but which really distorts the principles of the word of God.

They cause the Church to be removed from the "simplicity that is in Christ." The word "simplicity" has a variety of meanings

27

all of which help us to understand the operations of false apostolic ministry. The word means: *singleness of purpose without the duality of hypocrisy, absence of self-seeking, openness of heart manifesting in liberality and generosity.* It is this sincerity and wholesomeness of purpose ministered by the true apostles that the false ministers seek to compromise.

Their ministry corrupts the simplicity in the hearts of the believer. The word "corrupt" is *'phtheiro': to wash away, to wither, shrivel and dry up.* This is the same word used in *1 Corinthians 15:33:*

> *Do not be deceived: "Evil company corrupts good habits."*

Thus the word also suggests a corrupting or a degeneration that comes through association with an influence. These verses describe the inner operation of false apostolic ministry as it breaks down the spiritual standards of a community that was once established in the 'virginity' and purity of accurate apostolic impartation.

The Error of Self-Transformation

At the center of the falsehood is the principle of self-transformation:

> ¹³ *For such are false apostles, deceitful workers, transforming themselves into apostles of Christ.*
> ¹⁴ *And no wonder! For Satan himself transforms himself into an angel of light.*
> ¹⁵ *Therefore it is no great thing if his ministers also transform themselves into ministers of righteousness, whose end will be according to their works.*
>
> **2 Corinthians 11: 13 – 15 NKJ**

Self-transformation is the opposite of the process that takes place in one who has been divinely sent. A sending of the Lord contains within it the divine power of transformation as the apostle is equipped by divine grace to perform the work that he is ordained to do in the will of the Lord. Paul's calling to the apostolic ministry is indicative of the powerful transforming nature of the apostolic call. In *Acts 26* Paul is brought before king Agrippa and he recounts the encounter with the Lord that resulted in the call to apostolic ministry:

12 *"While so engaged as I was journeying to Damascus with the authority and commission of the chief priests,*

13 *at midday, O King, I saw on the way a light from heaven, brighter than the sun, shining all around me and those who were journeying with me.*

14 *"And when we had all fallen to the ground, I heard a voice saying to me in the Hebrew dialect, 'Saul, Saul, why are you persecuting Me? It is hard for you to kick against the goads.'*

15 *"And I said, 'Who are You, Lord?' And the Lord said, 'I am Jesus whom you are persecuting.*

16 *'But get up and stand on your feet; for this purpose I have appeared to you, to appoint you a minister and a witness not only to the things which you have seen, but also to the things in which I will appear to you;' ..."*

Acts 26: 12 – 16 NKJ

The apostolic calling totally transforms Paul from a bitter Pharisee into one of the foremost apostles of the faith. By the calling of the Lord he is 'made' a minister of the gospel.

The false apostles have no such transformational encounter and calling from God; they are deceitful workers transforming

themselves into ambassadors of the Christ. They function not
after the pattern of divine technology but follow satanic
patterns, since Satan himself transforms himself into an angel
of light. Self-transformation is the deepest level of the satanic
pattern because it denies the will and the initiative of the Lord,
while at the same time posturing to do His will in the earth.

Bondage and Self-Exaltation

¹⁹ You gladly put up with fools since you are so wise!
*²⁰ In fact, you even put up with anyone who enslaves you or
exploits you or takes advantage of you or pushes himself
forward or slaps you in the face.*
²¹ To my shame I admit that we were too weak for that! ...

2 Corinthians 11: 1 9 – 21 NIV

Paul's words are dripping with sarcasm. The false apostles
openly exploit the church for their own benefit, taking
advantage of the saints, promoting themselves over and above
the measure given to them by God and yet the saints accept this
illegitimate state of affairs. By contrast Paul compares his
sacrifice and persecution, his heart and his motivation with the
self-serving wickedness of the false apostles. Paul by contrast as
the pattern apostle is motivated by concern and care for the
corporate community of the Church:

*Besides everything else, I face daily the pressure of my concern
for all the churches.*

2 Corinthians 11: 28 NIV

The authority of the apostolic function can lead to excess in
those whose hearts do not keep the standards of the Kingdom
of God, and who do not walk in the compassion of Christ. In *1*

Thessalonians Paul indicates that the true apostles are those who refuse to abuse the authority that comes with the calling:

> 6 *Nor did we seek glory from men, either from you or from others, when we might have made demands as apostles of Christ.*
> 7 *But we were gentle among you, just as a nursing mother cherishes her own children.*
> 8 *So, affectionately longing for you, we were well-pleased to impart to you not only the gospel of God, but also our own lives, because you had become dear to us.*
>
> **1 Thessalonians 2: 6 – 8 NKJ**

In the end, the test of the quality of the apostolic ministry coming to the church is in the character of the apostle demonstrated among the saints:

> 10 *You are witnesses, and so is God, of how holy, righteous and blameless we were among you who believed.*
> 11 *For you know that we dealt with each of you as a father deals with his own children,*
> 12 *encouraging, comforting and urging you to live lives worthy of God, who calls you into his kingdom and glory.*
>
> **1 Thessalonians 2: 10 – 12 NIV**

Demands Upon Global Apostolic Ministry

It is undeniable that the Spirit of God is extending the spheres of apostolic ministries to global dimensions across the earth. There is a single divine purpose for the entire earth:

> 26 *"...This is the purpose that is purposed against the whole earth, and this is the hand that is stretched out over all the nations.*

*27 For the LORD of hosts has purposed, and who will annul
it? His hand is stretched out, and who will turn it back?"*
Isaiah 14: 26 – 27 NKJ

There is a divine purpose for the whole earth, not several
fractured initiatives that compete with each other. This coherent
single purpose is fixed and unchangeable. It cannot be dis-
annulled or cancelled. It will emphatically search for a
generation of apostolic strength that will discern it, come into
agreement with it and release it into executive apostolic actions
across the earth.

The movement of God is towards a global expression of
Himself. The knowledge of the glory will cover the earth:
*For the earth will be filled with the knowledge of the glory of
the LORD, as the waters cover the sea.*
Habakkuk 2: 14 NKJ

This implies global expression of God's truth, power and intent
without the restriction imposed on the activity of apostolic
ministries by national and political boundaries, religious and
denominational limitations or economic, cultural and ethnic
barriers.
The discernment of the singleness of the purpose of God will
also cause to come to the apostolic leaders of the earth a
revelational demand to work in covenant with each other.
There has to be an initiative of the Spirit of God to cause the
growing apostolic networks across the nations of the earth to
come together in new and exciting thrusts of the Spirit to work
in harmony, agreement, trust and deep cooperation. That is my
dream!

We must pour the new wine into new wineskins! We cannot express the new frequencies and abilities of the Apostolic Reformation in the old mentalities and operating paradigms of the past from which we are desperately escaping. And so there has to be a definite migration to new standards of apostolic operation and expression in this move of God.

I would like to indicate here some of the false activities and attitudes that we have seen manifested in various parts of the earth in apostolic activity, which we must remove from our midst if we are to express the 'true' apostolic attitudes that will bring forth the glory of God in the nations of the earth.

Identifying False Apostolic Principles in Global Ministry

Compromising of clear principles of truth in expressing partnership and covenant
One of the most fundamental principles in the clear expression of the true apostolic ministry is that there has to be a powerful return to the honoring of the expressions of covenant. What we express with our mouths must be demonstrated by our actions. If we have to build for God and cover the earth with the knowledge of His glory we simply cannot afford to be uncertain of the covenant expressions of our brothers or be betrayed when their promises are not kept and their hearts have no foundation of truth.

A wonderful picture of the standards David built in his move towards the establishment of the kingdom is revealed in the book of 1 Chronicles. A number of mighty warriors, former supporters of Saul's regime, come out to pledge allegiance to David:

> [17] *And David went out to meet them, and answered and said to them, "If you have come peaceably to me to help me, my heart will be united with you; but if to betray me to my enemies, since there is no wrong in my hands, may the God of our fathers look and bring judgment."*
>
> [18] *Then the <u>Spirit came upon Amasai</u>, chief of the captains, and he said: "We are yours, O David; we are on your side, O son of Jesse! Peace, peace to you, and peace to your helpers! For your God helps you."*
>
> **1 Chronicles 12: 17 – 18 NKJ**

The key to covenant as expressed here is the powerful activity of the Spirit in the hearts of both David and the men who come to him. We must come in peace to help each other, and there must be no wrong in our hands as the Spirit brings us to clear places of covenant for God's purposes across the earth.

Men becoming 'hunters' of the word in the ministry of another in order to use that word for ambitious self-advancement

No one apostle or apostolic network has access to the total truth that God is speaking in the earth in this last thrust to the finish of His purpose. It is for this reason that in many places I have said that there is a Spirit-birthed initiative for *'apostolic equalization'* – the emergence of apostles from every quarter of the earth regardless of their origin or ethnicity, standing together in mutual respect and acceptance.

The direction of the Spirit towards covenant-related apostles and interlocked apostolic networks is a clear indication that the day of the individual superstar is finally and thankfully over, and the voice of the Lord is coming forth from a corporate context (a global community of apostles) rather than from an individual context (the single, charismatic superstar of the Church).

In this context of the total truth becoming an amalgam of the revelation of several apostles, we all have to declare what we know and share what comes from others. This demands that a high degree of integrity become the standard when we teach and preach that which came forth from the revelation of another.

False apostles draw near simply to plunder and prey like vultures upon the revelatory words of other apostles, which they take away and portray as their own. These stolen teachings become the subject of books and word-for-word plagiarism as they promote their profile in the minds of others. These false practices must be terminated in the Church of the last days. We must honor each other or the advance of the Kingdom comes to a sudden halt. We may have multiple books and dozens of tape albums but yet be a hindrance to the clarity of the advance of the Kingdom of God:

> 22 *"Many will say to Me in that day, 'Lord, Lord, have we not prophesied in Your name, cast out demons in Your name, and done many wonders in Your name?'*
> 23 *"And then I will declare to them, 'I never knew you; depart from Me, you who practice lawlessness!'*
> **Matthew 7: 22 – 23 NKJ**

False claims for global and territorial authority

We have already examined the matter of apostolic spheres and measures that are given by the Lord to His apostles. Not every apostle has a global mandate and international measure. If an extensive measure is not given by the Lord, then the apostle who utilizes the powers and influence systems of the earth to leverage himself into a position of influence is operating in the principles of the false.

I was told a story by a brother from India of a popular female preacher who went from the USA to India and created an immediate network of pastors and leaders because she pumped huge sums of money into the meeting, purchasing motor-scooters, television sets and airline tickets for the leaders to attend the meeting. This is nothing but bribery. The report is that such action has seriously damaged the church in that part of India because now the leaders are unwilling to cooperate with any ministry that does not seduce them with rich gifts.

Activities such as this create false measures that are not designed in the purposes of God. To construct an apostolic network on such a foundation is both dangerous and deceptive. Jesus spoke of the man who was a false builder, who built his house on the sand (*Matthew 7: 24 - 29*). The structure looked strong until the rains, the floods and the wind blasted it apart and threw it down.

Arbitrary creation of ministry teams in order to create structures not built over time by the Lord, and toleration of inaccurate joinings in order to enhance ministry profile
False apostolic ministry cannot submit itself to the time frames of the Lord principally because of two reasons. It is either not 'sent', or is in a state of active rebellion against the rigorous application of the Kingdom principles which determine the standards of the apostolic ministry. Many times because of our very limited human point of view, it seems that the Lord is inactive and moving much too slowly to implement His final plans and purposes for the earth:

8 But, beloved, do not forget this one thing, that with the Lord one day is as a thousand years, and a thousand years as one day.

9 The Lord is not slack concerning His promise, as some count slackness, but is longsuffering toward us, not willing that any should perish but that all should come to repentance.

2 Peter 3: 8 – 9 NKJ

Because of this many who have not submitted to the sovereignty of the Lord, race ahead in plans of their own choosing. The slow road to covenant does not appeal to them and so they broker relationships with people not chosen by God to form global ministry teams, placing inaccurate representatives in several nations.

Extremism in doctrine and lack of balance and focus on Christ
Paul continually spoke of the false teachers, preachers and apostles who invaded the ranks of the Church with false teaching and doctrine. Indeed, one of the primary tasks of the

apostles is to clarify, adjust and establish doctrine so that the church can walk on a firm foundation:

> *42 And they continued steadfastly in the apostles' doctrine and fellowship, in the breaking of bread, and in prayers.*
>
> *43 Then fear came upon every soul, and many wonders and signs were done through the apostles.*
>
> *Acts 2: 42 – 43 NKJ*

Paul talks of dangers among false brothers *(2 Corinthians 11: 26)*. In the epistle to the Galatians, Paul speaks again of the false brethren who operate freely in the Church and cause the saints to be brought to a place of bondage:

> *4 And this occurred because of false brethren secretly brought in (who came in by stealth to spy out our liberty which we have in Christ Jesus, that they might bring us into bondage),*
>
> *5 to whom we did not yield submission even for an hour, that the truth of the gospel might continue with you.*
>
> *Galatians 2: 4 – 5 NKJ*

It is in this context that he openly has the famous clash with Peter over hypocrisy and false apostolic positions after brothers came down from James to the church at Antioch *(Galatians 2: 9 – 12)*. Peter had been eating with the Gentiles until the Jewish brothers came and then both he and Barnabas separated themselves from the Gentiles in a backward movement into religion, fear and corrupt doctrine. Paul's immediate and public confrontation of Peter is one of the clearest and most dramatic patterns for the struggle of the apostolic for integrity in doctrine.

To Apostle John the corruption of doctrine that was firmly based and focused on Christ was the manifestation of the spirit of antichrist:

7 For many deceivers have gone out into the world who do not confess Jesus Christ as coming in the flesh. This is a deceiver and an antichrist.

8 Look to yourselves, that we do not lose those things we worked for, but that we may receive a full reward.

9 Whoever transgresses and does not abide in the doctrine of Christ does not have God. He who abides in the doctrine of Christ has both the Father and the Son.

10 If anyone comes to you and does not bring this doctrine, do not receive him into your house nor greet him;

11 for he who greets him shares in his evil deeds.

2 John 1: 7 – 11 NKJ

The formation of Christ within the life of the believer is the apostolic intent:

My little children, for whom I labor in birth again until Christ is formed in you, …

Galatians 4: 19 NKJ

The word "formed" is *'morphoo'* and it refers to the creation of moral excellence within the life of the believer that comes after the experience of redemption by receiving Jesus. The application of this value to the corporate life of the global Church is the territory of the apostolic. No apostolic impartation is valid unless it brings the believers to a deeper formation of the Christ values on the inside of them.

Lack of emphasis on the necessity for personal transformation in the Apostolic Reformation, thus causing a diminishing of its power and reality in the earth

The power of a Reformation is in the dimension of structural change that takes place within the Church. The word "reformation" is found in *Hebrews 9: 10* in the context of the vast and structural change of God's order from the principles of the Law to the reality and experience of New Testament grace.

The word is *'diorthosis'* and it indicates a making straight or a bringing back into alignment of things that have become crooked or misaligned. The meaning of the word clearly indicates a structural operation taking place. It refers to the creation of outer order and beauty by the forceful adjustment of the internal shape and reality of things.

Thus, a Reformation is a return to the emphasis on inward structural change. There can be no Reformation without the proclamation of the need for spiritual activity to move inward instead of outward; without clarity that the outer life is shaped by spiritual value on the inside. When a Reformation emphasizes the outer rather than the inner, then the spirit of that Reformation is false.

Jeremiah saw prophetically the spiritual direction and emphasis of the most profound Reformation that has ever occurred – the movement from Law to Grace and he expressed it in this way:

> *"...But this is the covenant that I will make with the house of Israel after those days, says the LORD: I will put My law in*

their minds, and write it on their hearts; and I will be their God, and they shall be My people. ..."

Jeremiah 31: 33 NKJ

God's Reformation direction has always been to a more profound expression of Himself in the inner man.

The true apostolic message will always declare the need for personal change and the demand for greater clarity and accuracy in spiritual life. The apostle is not divorced from the message he declares. He both speaks and ultimately manifests the message. The cry coming forth from Paul was *'Imitate me!'* (1 Corinthians 4:16 / 11:1).

The danger of the false in the earth today is the strong declaration of a message which expresses principles and knowledge of Reformation, but leaves the basic structures of the Church unchanged. Such a message is the expression of the false apostolic.

The story of king Manasseh is the story of an apparent Reformation that had a false inner principle. Manasseh is a rotten king who destroys the moral structure of Judah. He practices witchcraft and sorcery. He causes his sons to pass through the fire in satanic rituals *(2 Chronicles 33:5 – 9)*. As a result he is defeated by the king of Assyria and taken to Babylon in captivity. Under the harshness of the imprisonment he 'repents' and God brings him back to Judah. He does institute some changes in things on his return but the deep structural change is never effected:

> ^{15} *He took away the foreign gods and the idol from the house of the LORD, and all the altars that he had built in the mount of the house of the LORD and in Jerusalem; and he cast them out of the city.*
>
> ^{16} *He also repaired the altar of the LORD, sacrificed peace offerings and thank offerings on it, and commanded Judah to serve the LORD God of Israel.*
>
> ^{17} *Nevertheless the people still sacrificed on the high places, but only to the LORD their God.*
>
> **2 Chronicles 33: 15 - 17 NKJ**

At the end of his process the people continue the offending sacrifice but now cosmetically name their sacrifice as unto God – outer change is seen but no inner transformation is made. This is the false reformation of the false apostolic.

The demand of the Apostolic Reformation is for proclaimers not 'echoes'. An echo is one who hears the word of Reformation and is stirred emotionally on the surface life of his soul. He then goes out to become not a genuine proclaimer – speaking out of the profundity of personal change and encounter with God, but an echo simply reflecting that which has no power to cause transformation in others. The true apostolic is seen and heard not in the lack of substance of the echo, but in the trumpet of the proclaimer of personal change.

The Accuracy of Paul's Response

> *And I will keep on doing what I am doing in order to cut the ground from under those who want <u>an opportunity to be considered equal with us</u> in the things they boast about.*
>
> *2 Corinthians 11: 12 NIV*

The false demands to be equal with the true. They can see the work and activity of the true apostolic and they demand that they be given the same recognition by others. Paul's principle for exposing that which was false was to continue to strongly operate in the principles which he had built in his ministry in order to "cut the ground" from under the ministries of the false apostles.

Let us consider several principles for apostolic operation in the ministry of Paul found in 2 *Corinthians,* and in so doing we are describing principles to be built in us, that will oppose and restrict the manifestation of the false in the earth.

Principles of the True Apostles from 2 Corinthians

<u>Principle One</u>: Thorough manifestation of the apostolic character (2 Corinthians. 11: 6)
This is a ministry dynamic that is very important. The apostle must be 'made visible' or 'become totally seen' in the perception of the people he ministers to. There can be no attempt to shield or to 'hide' the nature of his heart from the people.

43

2 Corinthians 6: 11 TLB
Oh, my dear Corinthian friends! I have told you all my feelings; I love you with all my heart.

2 Corinthians 6: 11 NIV
We have spoken freely to you, Corinthians, and opened wide our hearts to you.

Those who hear the word coming forth from the apostle must come to the realization that there is no gap between the content of the word and the position of the heart. Much more than simply the speaking of the accurate word, the true apostle ministers also the content of his heart and the reality of his life to those who receive him:

> 6 *Nor did we seek glory from men, either from you or from others, when we might have made demands as apostles of Christ.*
> 7 *But we were gentle among you, just as a nursing mother cherishes her own children.*
> 8 *So, affectionately longing for you, we were well <u>pleased to impart to you not only the gospel of God, but also our own lives</u>, because you had become dear to us*
> **1 Thessalonians 2: 6 – 8 NKJ**

<u>*Principle Two*</u>: *Correct financial activity*
(2 Corinthians 11: 7 – 9)
In many cases the arrival of apostolic ministry into a jurisdiction is caused not by an invitation being issued, but because he has been sent by the Lord to invade a region. For the true apostles of the Apostolic Reformation, financial gain is the very last thing on their minds.

The global Church has become used to ministries entering in with greed, calling for offering after offering, utilizing the most disgusting methods to extract the last dollar from the pockets of the poor victims unfortunate enough to come under their influence. Paul describes these as false apostles who are 'takers' not givers:

> *For you put up with it if one brings you into bondage, if one devours you, if one takes from you, if one exalts himself, if one strikes you on the face.*
>
> ### 2 Corinthians 11: 20 NKJ

By contrast the emphasis of Paul was to find ways not to be a burden to the saints at Corinth. In fact in Corinth Paul preached free of charge. These standards of ministry based on integrity are returning to the church as it enters deeply into an apostolic dimension.

Principle Three: *Emphasis on clear revelation*
(2 Corinthians 11: 6)

Paul's emphasis was not upon the artistry of his words or the eloquence of delivery but upon the development of revelation knowledge. Today in the Church around the earth we have inherited a method of delivery that assumes success if the people are brought to a shout at the end of every sentence and the preaching is punctuated by screams, cheers, jumping, shaking and crying. The emphasis is so heavily upon an emotional response, that in many cases the minds of the people are not touched at all as they respond entirely on a soulish and emotional level.

Paul's preaching was of the wisdom of God in a mystery:

> ⁴ *And my speech and my preaching were not with persuasive words of human wisdom, but in demonstration of the Spirit and of power,*
>
> ⁵ *that your faith should not be in the wisdom of men but in the power of God.*
>
> ⁶ *However, we speak wisdom among those who are mature, yet not the wisdom of this age, nor of the rulers of this age, who are coming to nothing.*
>
> ⁷ *But we speak the wisdom of God in a mystery, the hidden wisdom which God ordained before the ages for our glory, ...*
>
> **1 Corinthians 2: 4 – 7 NKJ**

Principle Four: Emphasis on serving rather than status (2 Corinthians 11: 22 – 23)

> ²² *Are they Hebrews? So am I. Are they Israelites? So am I. Are they the seed of Abraham? So am I.*
>
> ²³ *Are they ministers of Christ?-- I speak as a fool-- I am more: in labors more abundant, in stripes above measure, in prisons more frequently, in deaths often.*
>
> **2 Corinthians 11: 22 – 23 NKJ**

Paul is comparing his value to that of the false apostles who were coming into the churches in his day and he uses two levels of evaluation to discriminate between his level and theirs – status and serving.

The factor that separates Paul from the counterfeit was in the dimension of serving that he entered into. As a minister of

Christ, he says, "I am more." His service is "more abundant", "above measure" and "more frequent". It is in this clear demonstration in his ministry, of his commitment to paying the high personal price for the apostolic word in the Church, that Paul is separated from that which is also of the seed of Abraham, but falls short in the depth of the ministry of Christ.

Principle Five: Boasting in infirmity
(2 Corinthians 11: 30 / 12: 9 - 10)
In the apostolic paradigm, the clearer the realization and the revelation of personal weakness, the more access is given to the powerful dimension of divine grace. Apostolic revelation does not puff up with pride or conviction of personal cleverness.

The abundance of Paul's revelations caused a "thorn in the flesh" or a satanic messenger to buffet him in oppositions, resistances, persecutions, reverses, trials, imprisonments and abandonment, yet the grace of the Lord prevailed. This statement by Paul cuts across many of the attitudes of today's church in which material elegance, success and an almost humanistic persuasion of the power of the good time, has blunted the edge of the believer's perception of and access to the mighty grace of the Lord.

This grace or divine enabling resource is fundamental and basic to the working of the apostolic building capability. Jesus says to Paul: 'My strength is made perfect in weakness.' *(2 Corinthians 12:9).*

In the book of Zechariah, Zerubbabel represents a dimension of apostolic ministry charged with the task of rebuilding the temple and restoring the walls. The command of the Lord to Zerubbabel is that the temple cannot be constructed by might or power but by the activation of the Spirit of God:

> *⁶ So he answered and said to me: "This is the word of the LORD to Zerubbabel: 'Not by might nor by power, but by My Spirit,' says the LORD of hosts.*
>
> *⁷ 'Who are you, O great mountain? Before Zerubbabel you shall become a plain! And he shall bring forth the capstone with shouts of "Grace, grace to it!"' "*
>
> *⁸ Moreover the word of the LORD came to me, saying:*
>
> *⁹ 'The hands of Zerubbabel have laid the foundation of this temple; his hands shall also finish it. Then you will know that the LORD of hosts has sent Me to you.'*
>
> **Zechariah 4: 6 – 9 NKJ**

Paul's attitude is radically different from the attitudes of ministry today. He seeks as a priority the release of that grace into his life, so much so that he actually "takes pleasure" in infirmities and rejoices in persecutions and reproaches because he knows that this is the pathway to the awesome grace of God.

Principle Six: Correct projection of apostolic identity

> *For though I might desire to boast, I will not be a fool; for I will speak the truth. But I refrain, lest anyone should think of me above what he sees me to be or hears from me.*
>
> **2 Corinthians 12: 6 NKJ**

The issue here is the distortion of substance into image. Paul is careful that the saints are not led into an inaccurate concept of him and his ministry. He does not want anyone to think of him above what he sees or hears Paul to be. These apostolic positions are of particular emphasis in the modern world of today in which technology has the capability to boost image to unparalleled levels. The use of websites and the internet can project any concepts we wish into cyberspace and into the hearts of men across the earth.

More than ever before, as more and more powerful technology affords the Church even more opportunities to descend into marketing, false projections of public relations hype and downright dishonesty, we have to hold up and remember the apostolic standard.

In the end the mark of the true apostle is deep inside the heart. Paul constantly leads us away from looking at the exterior status, external comparison of ministries and inaccurate image in the eyes of men. The operation of the true apostle is built upon the cry from his heart for the churches of Jesus Christ in all the earth. It is this strong compassion and concern for the state of the global church that defines his position as ultimately true:

> *...besides the other things, what comes upon me daily: my deep concern for all the churches.*
>
> **2 Corinthians 11: 28 NKJ**

THREE

BENEFITS OF
THE APOSTOLIC I
Fundamental Principles

*A*s indicated before the apostle imparts the qualities that are part of his anointing and spiritual technology. He imparts an apostolic spirit or an apostolic dimension to the church. In considering the benefits of apostolic ministry, we are seeking to examine the components of that impartation of apostolic grace or apostolic resource.

The apostle is a 'conduit' for a massive inflow of divine life to the Church. The Webster definition describes a <u>conduit</u> as "a channel through which something (like a fluid) is conveyed." It is also described as "a means of transmitting or distributing". We can use a very simple but graphic example to more clearly capture the functionality of apostolic transmission. Imagine a gardener wishes to water her rosebushes. She attaches a rubber hose to the water faucet and points the end of the hose at the rosebush. When the tap is opened the hose (conduit) transfers the water through the length of the hose and deposits it where the gardener wants the water to truly go – to the rosebush. In fact, if you smell the water flowing out of the end of the rubber hose you will find that it carries a faint trace of the smell and taste of the rubber through which it passes.

In the same way God wants to deposit divine life and reality into the hearts and lives of the saints in the earth and he uses the apostles (and the rest of the governmental ministries) as conduits to transfer the unique dimension of the apostolic nature of Christ from the heavenly realms into the hearts and lives of the people of God in the earth.

The pure divine grace that flows through the life of the apostle interacts powerfully with the characteristics of the spiritual life of the particular apostle and so the apostolic grace that empties out of his life carries the spiritual temperament, personality, characteristics, experiences, spiritual processes and 'taste' of the individual apostle's life. It is therefore mandatory that for a full benefit to be brought to the Church, the life of the apostle must be thoroughly processed and deeply purified by the working of the Spirit of the Lord. This is the way Paul said it:

> 7 *But we have this treasure in earthen vessels that the excellence of the power may be of God and not of us.*
> 8 *We are hard-pressed on every side, yet not crushed; we are perplexed, but not in despair;*
> 9 *persecuted, but not forsaken; struck down, but not destroyed* –
> 10 *always carrying about in the body the dying of the Lord Jesus, that the life of Jesus also may be manifested in our body.*

> ¹¹ *For we who live are always delivered to death for Jesus' sake,*
> *that the life of Jesus also may be manifested in our mortal flesh.*
> ¹² *So then death is working in us, but life in you.*
>
> **2 Corinthians 4: 7 – 12 NKJ**

It was clear that the profound spiritual processes taking place in the life of Paul were designed by God to "press" Paul so that through the powerful purification of his life which he calls "death working in us" that spiritual life might flow powerfully and strongly to the saints under his care.

One cannot overstate the importance and vital nature of this transference or sharing of life from the apostle to the saints. This is what we call – *'the apostolic dimension'* – and this was impressed upon my mind and spirit in a very significant way by the Lord. Let me tell you a story from my own life.

Many years ago I was visiting a church led by a very powerful old apostle in the United States. The ministry of this old man had developed over very many years and now in his eighties he had feeding programs in developing nations and massive reputation across the earth. I sat in his camp-meeting as he ministered and laid his hands with prayer on the people gathered that day. I began to notice things. All the ushers in the building were quite elderly people. The worship leader in the meeting was quite old and the majority of the people gathered for the meeting were elderly themselves. I was very struck by the significant lack of younger people in the building and as I was musing on this suddenly I found myself in the Spirit, out of the building, in mid-air and gazing at a most fantastic scene.

I saw in the middle of the air a huge dragon just like those fire-breathing dragons of old European fairy tales. He was massive and very intimidating and I could sense his temperament and his attitude within my own being. It was as if I could clearly and easily track what was his intent at that time. His jaws were wide open and he was enraged and floating in mid-air between his open jaws was the dome structure of the church building I was sitting in at the time. The intent of the dragon – a clear representation of destructive satanic power – was to snap his jaws shut and crush the church and the old apostle's ministry entirely. He was consumed with hatred for the man and what he represented in the earth and in the Spirit. The beast was straining and struggling to clamp his jaws shut but they were kept forced open by the power of the personal apostolic grace upon that man of God. I saw the tension and struggle in the mind of the beast, but I also saw and felt his deep resolve that he would wait, straining to shut his open jaws, until the old apostle died and then he would completely destroy the apostolic mission flowing in that church.

I understood with startling clarity that the old apostle had never consciously transferred the massive grace upon him unto the people. He had not raised up another generation of effective young ministers in his church and had functioned only in the power of his own personal grace. Now the enemy would wait until he was dead and move in for the kill. I heard the voice of God speaking with a human voice clearly in my ear – "Never let this happen to you!" It has become my personal focus as one of the apostles of the modern Church to do all in my power to cause widespread transference, distribution and transmission of the grace that God has placed on my life and to bring direct and precise benefit to the Body of Christ in the earth. The words "apostle" and "benefit" flow very closely together.

If great benefit has to come to the Body of Christ from the apostolic resources given by God, there has to be full and conscious implementation of two broad areas of operations viz:
a) Powerful Releasing from the apostle;
b) Conscious Receiving by the Church.

Powerful Releasing

Release must occur in four areas:
- Recognition of the primary constituents of the gift;
- Search and enquiry for effective means of distribution;
- Development of character;
- Commitment to development.

Recognition of the primary constituents of the gift
Each apostle is different from any other. Each apostle has his own unique temperament in the Spirit; has a unique spiritual journey and process that led him to the place of full functionality and empowerment in the gift; has unique and individually peculiar ways and styles of expressing or outputting the gift that resides in his life. The *'process of the call'* is very important in the defining of the special and individual technology of the apostolic gift. Let us look at the experience of apostle Paul.

Saul the Pharisee is on his way to the city of Damascus in Syria. He is hunting and persecuting believers in Jesus in every city in the region. He describes in his own words the mission in which he was engaged:

> ¹⁰ *This I also did in Jerusalem, and many of the saints I shut up in prison, having received authority from the chief priests; and when they were put to death, I cast my vote against them.*
> ¹¹ *And I punished them often in every synagogue and compelled them to blaspheme; and being exceedingly enraged against them, I persecuted them even to foreign cities*
>
> *Acts 26: 10 – 11 NKJ*

On his way to Damascus he has a traumatic and life-changing direct encounter with Jesus. A light that was brighter than the sun at mid-day shone from heaven upon Saul and he fell to the ground blinded by the intensity of the revealed glory of the Lord (*Acts 26:13–14*). This is the moment of transformation in Saul's life. From this point he will be put in a spiritual process by the Lord that will make him Paul the apostle. The change of his name indicates the far-reaching developmental changes initiated by the Lord in his life. We are present at the actual moment of the first massive infusion of divine grace as the future apostolic DNA is coded into Paul's spirit. It is the voice of the Lord into Paul's life that carries with it the deep internal renovation and alignment of his grace for future ministry and function:

> ¹⁶ … *'But rise and stand on your feet; for I have appeared to you for this purpose, to make you a minister and a witness both of the things which you have seen and of the things which I will yet reveal to you.*
> ¹⁷ *'I will deliver you from the Jewish people, as well as from the Gentiles, to whom I now send you,*

---

[18] *'to open their eyes, in order to turn them from darkness to light, and from the power of Satan to God, that they may receive forgiveness of sins and an inheritance among those who are sanctified by faith in Me.'*

Acts 26: 16 – 18 NKJ

Jesus initiates the spiritual process. He will "make (Paul) a minister", and he encodes the specific and peculiar primary technology of Paul's apostolic gifting. He sends him *(the apostolic impartation)* to "open their eyes" and to "turn them from darkness to light". He will make him a witness of what he has "seen" and of the things that he will in the future "reveal".

The combination of words in the language used by the Lord indicate the nature of the functionality of the apostolic grace descending on Paul – sight; opening of eyes; revelation; turning from darkness to light. Paul is to be a revelation apostle – this will be the strength of the grace that he will distribute. He will be given the power to banish darkness and to cause revelatory sight to be imparted to the saints. He will become the primary revelation apostle of the day writing letters to the churches and defining the doctrine upon which the structures of the early Church will be built. More than the writings of any other apostle his writings will form the major part of the New Testament of the Bible.

It is clear in Paul's writings that he is completely aware of this new 'empowerment' given to him. His great impartation prayer over the apostolic center at Ephesus indicates his sharp and clear appreciation for the technology of his apostolic gift:

15 Therefore I also, after I heard of your faith in the Lord Jesus and your love for all the saints,

16 do not cease to give thanks for you, making mention of you in my prayers: 17 that the God of our Lord Jesus Christ, the Father of glory, may give to you the spirit of wisdom and revelation in the knowledge of Him,

18 the eyes of your understanding being enlightened; that you may know what is the hope of His calling, what are the riches of the glory of His inheritance in the saints ...

Ephesians 1: 15 – 18 NKJ

He zeroes in on the primary apostolic requirement of this new church - revelation and sight through the opening of the eyes of the heart. The blinding of his natural eyes on the road to Damascus was symbolic of the opening of his spiritual eyes and the opening of his spiritual understanding and now he is aware that he can impart the same quality of experience to those to whom he ministers:

8 To me, who am less than the least of all the saints, this grace was given, that I should preach among the Gentiles the unsearchable riches of Christ,

9 and to make all see what is the fellowship of the mystery, which from the beginning of the ages has been hidden in God who created all things through Jesus Christ;

10 to the intent that now the manifold wisdom of God might be made known by the church to the principalities and powers in the heavenly places,

Ephesians 3: 8 – 10 NKJ

He is aware that he has received a "grace" and that this grace can "make all see". The word used in the original Greek is *'photizo' – to shed rays of light; to cause illumination to be given.* It is the word that forms the root of the word 'photograph'. It suggests the development of an image through the giving of light. Paul through the grace can cause to form in the minds and hearts of people a new picture or a new revelation level of understanding in the mysteries of the Lord. He has the grace-filled power to do that as a benefit to those he ministers unto.

In order for maximum benefit to flow to the Church from the apostolic gift, the apostle has to be aware of what is the foundational competency of the grace he has been given and become skilled in the accurate release and utilization of the grace. In this way great blessing flows outward to the Body of Christ.

Search and enquiry for effective means of distribution

Further to recognizing the nature of the apostolic grace functioning through his life, the apostle must engage in search or enquiry for the most effective means for the grace to flow completely off him and into the lives of those to whom he ministers.

In order for maximum benefit to be received by the saints every possible method of the delivery of ministry must be studied and made more effective and efficient in the life of the apostle. These will include:

- *The design of events at which the apostle ministers:*
Incorrect design can compromise the effectiveness of the flow of the grace outwards and weaken the strength of the apostolic impartation.

- *The precise nature of the utterance:*
The apostle has to keenly discover his own spiritual flow and stay strongly within the native frequency he has been given by the Lord. He must not be seduced into what is popular, crowd-pleasing or emotionally stimulating to the gathered people. He must discern the preference of the Lord for the particular apostolic flow to the people for that time and remain strictly within the definitions of the Lord.

- *Discovery and development of correct personal strengths:*
There must be developed a seamless integration of the personal developments in the life of the apostle and the nature and definition of the grace that he carries. In this the apostle carries a great responsibility. If the grace that is upon him is intense, wisdom-filled and revelatory then the apostle in his personal life cannot pursue that which is frivolous, light or frothy. He must direct his natural mind and circumstances to be profound and weighty.

Selection of the right supporting ministers
For maximum benefit to flow to the saints the apostle must

carefully select the ministers that closely surround him and assist in the flow of the impartation to the people. Paul surrounded himself with suitable ministers who could "remind you of my ways in Christ" *(1 Corinthians 4:14b).* While there is variety in ministry expression, there must be uniformity and conformity in the nature of the quality of the grace that flows from the apostle and the apostolic or ministry team that functions together with him.

All of this care is taken to avoid "wastage" of the grace resource. The determination of the apostle is that the heavenly deposit be imparted completely to the lives of the saints in the Body of Christ. This was the determination and direction of the ministry of Jesus Christ. He always sought to benefit those he ministered unto by full and complete disclosure and impartation of the grace given to him by the Father:

> *No longer do I call you servants, for a servant does not know what his master is doing; but I have called you friends, for all things that I heard from My Father I have made known to you.*
> **John 15: 15 NKJ**

Development of character
If one tracks through Paul's ministry and his writing to the churches it becomes clear that in his mind there was a firm link between the quality of his character and the effectiveness of his apostolic gift. The two could not be separated. For maximum benefit to be brought to the lives of the saints the life of the apostle delivering the grace was to be as structurally sound and architecturally beautiful as the grace itself.

Paul's letters and exhortations to the saints at Thessalonica are
instructive:

> *For our gospel did not come to you in word only, but also in*
> *power, and in the Holy Spirit and in much assurance, as you*
> *know what kind of men we were among you for your sake.*
>
> *1 Thessalonians 1: 5 NKJ*

The effectiveness of the ministry depended on what "kind of
men" they were or what sort of life they demonstrated in the
city among the believers. They were effective and transparent
in their ministry while they stayed there and it was for the
saints' sake or for their benefit.

> ² *For neither at any time did we use flattering words, as you*
> *know, nor a cloak for covetousness – God is witness.*
>
> ³ *Nor did we seek glory from men, either from you or from*
> *others, when we might have made demands as apostles of*
> *Christ.*
>
> ⁴ *But we were gentle among you, just as a nursing mother*
> *cherishes her own children.*
>
> ⁵ *So, affectionately longing for you, we were well-pleased to*
> *impart to you not only the gospel of God, but also our own*
> *lives, because you had become dear to us.*
>
> *1 Thessalonians 2: 5 – 8 NKJ*

Their rank as apostles would have made it possible for them to
make demands on the people, but the counterbalancing reality
of developed lifestyles and total commitment to Christ-like
character caused a presentation of 'total' apostolic ministry. In
the end, Paul says, they imparted not only the gospel of God
but they also imparted their own lives and character to the
people.

Commitment to development
Increased productivity of the apostolic grace within the Body of Christ requires continuous and increased development in the life of the apostle himself. Paul's spiritual posture was one in which the pursuit of personal development and spiritual growth was a key feature of his life:

> ¹² *Not that I have already obtained all this, or have already been made perfect, but I press on to take hold of that for which Christ Jesus took hold of me.*
> ¹³ *Brothers, I do not consider myself yet to have taken hold of it. But one thing I do: Forgetting what is behind and straining toward what is ahead,*
> ¹⁴ *I press on toward the goal to win the prize for which God has called me heavenward in Christ Jesus.*
> ¹⁵ *All of us who are mature should take such a view of things. And if on some point you think differently, that too God will make clear to you.*
>
> **Philippians 3: 12 – 15 NIV**

This was not a casual movement forward. He uses the words "press" and "straining towards what is ahead". The call of God is heavenward – that is the direction of the motivation of the grace that is upon his life and thus the apostle himself must configure his desires, his efforts, his motivations, his eager pursuit of knowledge and understanding of God's ways in similar direction. Paul describes this attitude as the foundation of maturity.

This attitude and pursuit serves as a pattern for the spiritual walk and posture of all the saints. The apostle is aware that his alignment carries patterns that the Church should walk in and empowers them to discern that which is deviant and inaccurate. Thus the accurate spiritual pursuit of the apostle empowers the Church into correct levels of discernment.

Brethren, join in following my example, and note those who so walk, as you have us for a pattern.

Philippians 3: 17 NKJ

Conscious Receiving

Achieving effective apostolic benefit can be described as a push-pull situation. In the 'push' part of the equation we have seen that the apostle has to be conscious of all the components of effective ministry. He has to have awareness of the nature and the architecture of the grace given to him by the Lord and also has to submit to thorough processing by the Lord in his own life and personal structure to ensure that there is a seamless alignment of the grace with the life through which the grace flows.

On the 'pull' side those receiving the apostolic grace have a great responsibility to be conscious and aware of how they position themselves to receive from the Lord through the apostolic grace. Jesus warned the people about the general principle of careful and aware receiving:

"...Therefore take heed how you hear. For whoever has, to him more will be given; and whoever does not have, even what he seems to have will be taken from him."

Luke 8: 18 NKJ

Inaccurate or careless receiving can cause you to be robbed of even the small previous impartation that you received. We can say that careless receiving makes the believer 'leaky' and incapable of sustaining the grace that he has received from the Lord. Let us look at a few of the requirements for effective receiving of the apostolic grace. They are:

- Application of correct discernment;
- Removal of personal and ministry contaminants;
- Honoring of the apostolic grace;
- Strong personal conviction in the heart.

Application of correct discernment
Many things can distort the inflow of the apostolic word and ministry into the heart – strong embedded traditional concepts; nationalistic and ethnic biases; fundamental ignorance of biblical truth; inaccurate self-concept and ministry concept; unconquered personal fears and conditions of basic distrust; arrogance, pride and ego; and the list goes on and on.

The end result is that the capacity to correctly discern or to "see correctly into" the nature of the apostle and the grace that he brings is limited. Sight is very important. It is the beginning of the 'hand' that reaches out to grasp divine destiny that is being offered. This is what God said to Abraham as he upgraded his divine destiny after he separated from Lot:

14 *The LORD said to Abram after Lot had parted from him,
"Lift up your eyes from where you are and look north and south, east and west.*
15 *"All the land that you see I will give to you and your offspring forever."*

Genesis 13: 14 – 15 NIV

All of his future advance is dependent upon what he sees and how much he sees. He must have complete all-round sight not tunnel vision. He has to look north, south, east and west. The extent and effectiveness of his sight is the trigger to God's giving. If Abraham is 'blind' or has impaired or incorrect seeing then he will gain nothing.

Our sight unlocks the power, accuracy and reach we have into the spirit realm. The power of the Holy Spirit comes to give us sight. The power of the enemy comes to blind us:

Satan, who is the god of this world, has blinded the minds of those who don't believe. They are unable to see the glorious light of the Good News. They don't understand this message about the glory of Christ, who is the exact likeness of God.

2 Corinthians 4: 4 NLT

This scripture is applied in the context of the work of the enemy producing resistance to the truth in unbelievers, but it does show what methods the "god of this world" uses. The word used for "blinded" is the Greek word *'tuphloo'* – *to blow smoke; to obscure;* and it indicates the operations of Satan in blinding or preventing sight which then produces inaccurate activity in the Spirit.

To receive the apostolic correctly we must have clear sight and must step beyond our limitations and biases to receive a new and fresh revelation and position from the Lord. In the end it requires a clearing and correction of the heart for as Jesus says:

Blessed are the pure in heart, for they will see God.

Matthew 5: 8

Removal of personal and ministry contaminants
On the individual level then sight is directly linked to personal purity. Sometimes this is a developmental process as the inflow of the apostolic impartation begins to reveal to us our true nature and limitations. It sometimes takes time to truly and clearly receive the apostolic as we move from one level of blindness to greater and greater sight. We can see this in the incident when Jesus laid his hands on a blind man:

> 23 *He took the blind man by the hand and led him outside the village. When he had spit on the man's eyes and put his hands on him, Jesus asked, "Do you see anything?"*
> 24 *He looked up and said, "I see people; they look like trees walking around."*
> 25 *Once more Jesus put his hands on the man's eyes. Then his eyes were opened, his sight was restored, and he saw everything clearly.*
>
> **Mark 8: 23 – 25 NKJ**

At first the apostolic grace impacting the inaccuracies within our own hearts and lives causes a confusion of sight. The transition from limited sight to clear spiritual sight can take some getting used to. At first it seems as if we see *"men like trees walking around"*. What an accurate description of the confusion of transition! But as the heart clears and sight comes fully to the emerging understanding, our spiritual eyes are opened and we *"see everything clearly"*.

The apostolic sight must come to our churches also, and here too there are corporate contaminants that prevent clear sight of the preferred destiny in God that is announced and transmitted to the Body through effective apostolic ministry. Many things can cause the corporate body to be blind to the apostolic grace:

- Absolutely wrong and unbiblical leadership structures;
- Strong development of self-indulgent and 'bless-me' culture in the church;
- Wrong concepts of 'ownership' of the ministry by the senior leadership;
- Fully developed materialistic mentalities in the church;
- Hero-worship of the Senior Pastor and placing him on an unbiblical pedestal;
- Undeveloped capacity of the church to receive teaching;
- Corporate over-emotionalism that prevents deep analysis and thought;
- Over emphasis on church services and no concept of spiritual building;
- Strong nationalistic mentalities that limit how the church receives.

Full receiving of the incoming apostolic grace requires all of these corporate contaminants to be identified and progressively removed. The apostolic grace moves the church towards the uniformity of Kingdom culture, attitudes and standards as provided in the Word of God. The apostolic grace does not submit itself to nationalistic preferences. We see that clearly and sharply indicated in Paul's confrontation of Peter when Peter bowed to the pressure of Jewish cultural preferences:

11 *When Peter came to Antioch, I opposed him to his face, because he was clearly in the wrong.*

12 *Before certain men came from James, he used to eat with the Gentiles. But when they arrived, he began to draw back and*

separate himself from the Gentiles because he was afraid of those who belonged to the circumcision group.

13 The other Jews joined him in his hypocrisy, so that by their hypocrisy even Barnabas was led astray.

14 When I saw that they were not acting in line with the truth of the gospel, I said to Peter in front of them all, "You are a Jew, yet you live like a Gentile and not like a Jew. How is it, then, that you force Gentiles to follow Jewish customs?"

Galatians 2: 11 – 14 NIV

"They were not acting in line with the truth of the gospel" – this is the apostolic standard and the cry in the heart of the more accurate and developed apostolic level of Paul. We can see that the correct receiving of the apostolic grace configures churches all across the world to move away from inaccurate nationalistic and ethnic standards towards the biblically defined Kingdom standards. This creates the commonality of Kingdom culture in the single Body of Christ all across the earth.

Honoring of the apostolic grace

When talking about honoring the apostolic grace I am not talking about flattery or empty praise. This is not the honoring of the flesh but the honoring of the Spirit that involves receiving the apostle properly with a correct attitude of recognition and honoring in the heart. Thus the honoring is primarily internal and spiritual but expresses itself in action and attitude.

Matthew 10 recounts the incredible incident when Jesus upgraded his disciples to the rank of apostles and first sent them out. He gives detailed and precise instructions that would form the operations patterns of their apostolic function. At the end of his time of instruction he releases this powerful principle:

> 40 *"He who receives you receives Me, and he who receives Me receives Him who sent Me.*
>
> 41 *He who receives a prophet in the name of a prophet shall receive a prophet's reward. And he who receives a righteous man in the name of a righteous man shall receive a righteous man's reward."*
>
> **Matthew 10: 40 - 41 NKJ**

Correct honoring and receiving of the apostle, sets up a direct line of impartation to the Father who sent Jesus. You can call this *'the upward connectivity of sent-ness'* – from the apostle in the earth through Jesus THE apostle directly to the One who 'sends' us all – the Father Above!

It is important, Jesus says, that those you go to correctly identify and correctly receive you. If one is received as a prophet then a prophet's reward is released. If one is received as only a righteous man than only a righteous man's reward is released. Correct identification of the nature of the grace that is coming into the church determines the level and quality of impartation that will come forth from God.

In Corinth, a church in which there was much spiritual gifting but also great disorder, transgression and confusion, Paul's apostolic grace was severely dishonored:

> 10 *"For his letters," they say, "are weighty and powerful, but his bodily presence is weak, and his speech contemptible"*

[11] *Let such a person consider this, that what we are in word by letters when we are absent, such we will also be in deed when we are present.*

2 Corinthians 10: 10 - 11 NKJ

They loved the teaching but rejected the teacher. They loved the spiritual outflow but cursed the vessel through which the outflow came. Inaccurate receiving produced a church full of chaos and deserving of judgment. Paul struggled with this church and at times instead of revelation and blessing his ministry moved to threat and judgment. This was not a good situation at all!

Strong personal conviction in the heart
It all comes back to the heart – the core of the reliable Kingdom experience:

Above all else, guard your heart, for it is the wellspring of life.

Proverbs 4: 23 NKJ

It is the condition of the heart that determines if the impact of the word of God and the grace of the Lord through the apostle's teaching and ministry is retained and increased or if it withers and dies. Jesus taught the people about the vital importance of the heart in the Parable of the Sower and the Seed. In the Parable the farmer walks through the field casting the seed upon the ground with variable results. Jesus explains the parable this way:

[11] *"This is the meaning of the parable: The seed is the word of God.*

¹² Those along the path are the ones who hear, and then the devil comes and takes away the word from their hearts, so that they may not believe and be saved.
¹³ Those on the rock are the ones who receive the word with joy when they hear it, but they have no root. They believe for a while, but in the time of testing they fall away.
¹⁴ The seed that fell among thorns stands for those who hear, but as they go on their way they are choked by life's worries, riches and pleasures, and they do not mature.
¹⁵ But the seed on good soil stands for those with a noble and good heart, who hear the word, retain it, and by persevering produce a crop."

Luke 8: 11 – 15 NIV

The spiritual transactions take place in the heart and the heart can be hard, shallow, infertile or deep, rich and productive. It is our choice to make. The apostolic ministry must be received with deep heart conviction. One must engage in prophetic enquiry concerning the identity of the apostolic grace determined by God to be the primary point of apostolic grace into the individual life and the corporate body. Once identified this apostolic grace must be received with joy, respect and profound conviction of heart.

FOUR

BENEFITS OF

THE APOSTOLIC II
Imparting Wisdom
Establishing Government

I
Imparting Wisdom

We must remember that the apostle imparts the spiritual qualities that are part of his anointing and operational technology. He imparts an apostolic spirit or an apostolic dimension to the Church. This is extremely important. *Ephesians 4: 12* indicates that the apostles have been sent by the Lord for the purpose of "equipping" the saints. The word used for "equipping" or perfecting is *'katartismos'* It is the word from which the English word 'artisan' is derived and it carries the concept of *a craftsman molding or carving out a shape of art or beauty out of a block of raw material.* The skillful craftsman, the apostle, shapes out a perfected shape of the original faith according to an already approved standard, which is Christ Jesus Himself. Thus the work defines the fundamental work of the apostolic gift.

In considering the benefits of the apostolic ministry we are seeking to examine the components of that impartation of the apostolic grace or the apostolic resource. One of the most significant benefits that the apostle brings to the Church is the impartation of a spirit of wisdom.

The Apostle Imparts the Spirit of Wisdom

In *Luke Chapter 11* Jesus is in a state of high confrontation with the Pharisees:

> [49] *"Therefore the wisdom of God also said, 'I will send them prophets and apostles, and some of them they will kill and persecute,'*
> [50] *"that the blood of all the prophets which was shed from the foundation of the world may be required of this generation,..."*
> *Luke 11: 49 – 50 NKJ*

Jesus speaks of a future move of God as a solution to the corruption of the Pharisee spirit in the Church. He says, *"I will send ..."*, clearly indicating an initiative of the future and he also details the sequence in which the sending will take place – first the prophets and then the apostles. It is also clear that he could not be referring to the Old Testament prophets who were already history by the time Jesus spoke this; another prophetic dimension was being referred to.

These scriptures are being fulfilled in our time. In the 1980s there was a powerful release of prophetic dimension all across the earth in a move of God which became known as the Prophetic Move and in this time God is following up with a release of the apostolic as the prophetic words of Jesus are literally being confirmed before our very eyes.

In the book of Matthew this incident is recorded from another perspective:

34 *"Therefore, indeed, I send you prophets, wise men, and scribes: some of them you will kill and crucify, and some of them you will scourge in your synagogues and persecute from city to city, ..."*

Matthew 23: 34 NKJ

Here the apostles are called "wise men" and the core technology or the signature feature of the apostolic grace is identified – wisdom. Paul in speaking of the anointing that rested upon his life described himself in *1 Corinthians 3: 10* as a "wise master builder". I will speak more of this aspect of the apostolic in a later chapter.

There are several kinds of wisdom referred to in the Word of God. There is the natural wisdom which develops in one who has lived a long life in the earth and who has experienced much in his natural life:

12 *Wisdom is with aged men, and with length of days, understanding.*

Job 12: 12 NKJ

There is a wisdom which comes from study of the Word of God and application of the principles of the Kingdom:

> 7 *The law of the LORD is perfect, converting the soul; the testimony of the LORD is sure, making wise the simple;*
> 8 *The statutes of the LORD are right, rejoicing the heart; the commandment of the LORD is pure, enlightening the eyes;*
> **Psalm 19: 7 - 8 NKJ**

There is also a wisdom which is produced in human lives through the chastening and the correction processes of the Lord in one's life:

> 11 *My son, do not despise the chastening of the LORD, nor detest His correction;*
> 12 *For whom the LORD loves He corrects, just as a father the son in whom he delights.*
> 13 *Happy is the man who finds wisdom, and the man who gains understanding;*
> **Proverbs 3: 11 - 13 NKJ**

Finally, there is a wisdom which any believer can seek for and receive from the Lord which enables him to make correct choices in life and demonstrate this through the soberness and order of his life before men:

> *If any of you lacks wisdom, let him ask of God, who gives to all liberally and without reproach, and it will be given to him.*
> **James 1: 5 NKJ**

> 13 *Who is wise and understanding among you? Let him show by good conduct that his works are done in the meekness of wisdom.*

14 But if you have bitter envy and self-seeking in your hearts, do not boast and lie against the truth.

15 This wisdom does not descend from above, but is earthly, sensual, demonic.

16 For where envy and self-seeking exist, confusion and every evil thing are there.

17 But the wisdom that is from above is first pure, then peaceable, gentle, willing to yield, full of mercy and good fruits, without partiality and without hypocrisy.

James 3: 13 – 17 NKJ

All these aspects of wisdom are valuable and necessary for the complete spiritual life, but these dimensions of wisdom are grown and developed over time in the believer's life and are evidence of the increasing maturity of the faith in demonstration.

The wisdom that is evidenced in the apostolic gift, which we describe as the fundamental apostolic resource, is not a wisdom which has been manifested in the apostle's life either by time or by seeking God. It is a supernatural impartation by the sovereign will of God. Like all other governmental ministries the apostle must continue to grow personally and spiritually, and must continue to refine and polish the resource deposited in him by God, but apostolic wisdom is the raw material of his apostolic function.

Paul was the last person anyone would have chosen to be an apostle, but contrary to human reasoning and against human logic, God supernaturally arrests his life and releases what Paul can only call a "grace" that transforms him into a wise master-builder for God. This grace is so manifest that it can literally be perceived by the spiritually discerning apostles in Jerusalem when Paul visits to receive affirmation of his ministry to the Gentiles:

> ... *and when James, Cephas, and John, who seemed to be pillars, perceived the grace that had been given to me, they gave me and Barnabas the right hand of fellowship, that we should go to the Gentiles and they to the circumcised.*
>
> **Galatians 2: 9 NKJ**

The grace or the transforming power of supernatural wisdom was "given" not earned. It was sovereignly imparted not fasted or prayed for; it was received not taken; it was by the decision of God not the ordination and timing of man. It was what we can only call the spiritual substance of apostolic wisdom and is the basic empowerment of the apostolic position. This is what God poured in to make the apostle and it is what the apostle pours out when he in turn imparts the nature of his gifting to the receiving saints. Let us look more closely at some dimensions of this wisdom.

Wisdom is The Power to Build

> ***Proverbs 24: 3 - 4 NKJ***
> 3 *Through wisdom a house is built, and by understanding it is established;*
> 4 *By knowledge the rooms are filled with all precious and pleasant riches.*

Proverbs 9: 1 – 3 NKJ
¹ Wisdom has built her house, she has hewn out her seven pillars;
² She has slaughtered her meat, she has mixed her wine, she has also furnished her table.
³ She has sent out her maidens, she cries out from the highest places of the city,...

The word "house" here does not refer to a natural house of stone and mortar but to the spiritual construction of the "house of the Lord" or the corporate community of the Lord's people. Here wisdom and the building technology of the apostolic are represented as indicated by Paul in *1 Corinthians 3:10*. The ability to develop and construct the people of the Lord according to divine plan and purpose is a major thrust of apostolic resource. The house is established or made permanent by understanding. All the compartments of its spiritual operations and functions – its rooms – are filled by the release of the knowledge that comes with apostolic wisdom.

Apostolic wisdom creates perfected and complete structures in the Spirit represented here by the seven pillars that are literally hewn out. Seven is the number of completeness and the perfection of divine design in the structure. The spiritual structures developed by the impartation of apostolic resource are strong and firm as indicated by the creation of pillars in the design in *Proverbs 9:1*.

In the prophetic metaphor of the perfected spiritual house we see in *Proverbs Chapter 9*, the meat is slaughtered representing the release of a fresh revelation word of the Lord; the wine is mixed representing the accurate and skillful blending of the anointings needed to produce a "spiritual feast" in the house of the Lord; and the maidens cry from the highest places of the city representing the ability of the apostolic company of believers to proclaim the purposes of the Lord from the place of highest spiritual elevation in the jurisdiction in which they have been built. This is what the release of the apostolic grace, or the wisdom impartation, produces in the building of the house of the Lord. We must keep in mind that these scriptures describe the resources that are available to the corporate company in the release of the apostolic gift.

Wisdom is the Power of Spiritual Promotion

Proverbs 4: 7 – 9 NKJ
7 "... Wisdom is the principal thing; therefore get wisdom. And in all your getting, get understanding.
8 Exalt her, and she will promote you; she will bring you honor, when you embrace her.
9 She will place on your head an ornament of grace; a crown of glory she will deliver to you."

Proverbs 8: 11 NKJ
11 For wisdom is better than rubies, and all the things one may desire cannot be compared with her.

Proverbs 16: 16 NKJ
16 How much better to get wisdom than gold! And to get understanding is to be chosen rather than silver.

The value of wisdom is, above all, natural blessings. The writer uses the most valuable gems and metals of his day to demonstrate the simple fact that wisdom exceeds in value anything that can be identified on the earthly realm. But the power of wisdom in releasing spiritual virtue can only be manifested if wisdom is "exalted" and "embraced". Clear extreme value must be placed on the resource in the heart of the church and there must be an embracing of the value of the apostolic resource for the release of the 'promotion' to take place.

The apostolic resource does not degrade the church but brings honor to its "head". The word head speaks of rank and spiritual position which is enhanced by the impartation of the apostolic resource. An ornament of "grace" – *favor, elegance, charm and acceptance,* and a crown of "glory" – *beauty, splendor of rank and honor* will be imparted by the receiving and embracing of the pure impartation of the apostolic resource.

Unless the possibility of these fine spiritual values are understood, the Church of the 21st century will be unaware of the resources being released by God in this present Apostolic Reformation and will continue to walk in the low standard to which it has become accustomed. The apostolic ministry has been released not to enhance itself but to upgrade and beautify the Church with the revealed glory of God.

Wisdom is at The Heart of Territorial Warfare

Proverbs 21: 22 NIV
A wise man attacks the city of the mighty and pulls down the stronghold in which they trust.

Ecclesiastes 7: 19
Wisdom strengthens the wise more than ten rulers of the city.

The "city of the mighty" represents satanic stronghold positions in our jurisdictions and in our lives which previously have been unassailable. These are places we have been forced to retreat from in the battle for the purposes of God in the earth. The Church has been so incapable of ever breaching these satanic strongholds that now the enemy has developed a confidence in them. The release of the apostolic impartation causes the Church to be empowered to fight to a greater degree of spiritual effectiveness to literally attack these trusted strongholds and bring them down.

It is clear that the impartation of wisdom, the apostolic resource, positively adjusts the spiritual ranking of the corporate community. Released apostolic wisdom causes an impartation of spiritual strength which provides the Church with greater force to prevail; higher ranking in the spirit and ability to fight from a higher place; authority and validity of spiritual existence in the midst of the territory. The wise church is strengthened to a greater degree than ten spiritual rulers of the city. Thus the receiving, embracing and releasing of the apostolic resource makes the corporate company the territorial prince of its jurisdiction.

Wisdom is the Ability to Comprehend the Hidden Design

Proverbs 8: 22 - 31 NKJ

22 *"The LORD possessed me at the beginning of His way, before His works of old.*

23 *I have been established from everlasting, from the beginning, before there was ever an earth.*

24 *When there were no depths I was brought forth, when there were no fountains abounding with water.*

25 *Before the mountains were settled, before the hills, I was brought forth;*

26 *While as yet He had not made the earth or the fields, or the primeval dust of the world.*

27 *When He prepared the heavens, I was there, when He drew a circle on the face of the deep,*

28 *When He established the clouds above, when He strengthened the fountains of the deep,*

29 *When He assigned to the sea its limit, so that the waters would not transgress His command, when He marked out the foundations of the earth,*

30 *Then I was beside Him as a master craftsman; and I was daily His delight, rejoicing always before Him,*

31 *Rejoicing in His inhabited world, and my delight was with the sons of men."*

This is perhaps one of the most amazing scriptures in the entire bible. Here wisdom is personified as a woman who is speaking to us of her experience:

1 *Does not wisdom call out? Does not understanding raise her voice?*

2 On the heights along the way, where the paths meet, she takes her stand;
3 beside the gates leading into the city, at the entrances, she cries aloud:
4 "To you, O men, I call out; I raise my voice to all mankind."

Proverbs 8: 1 - 4 NIV

Personification or the presentation of abstract spiritual values in the form of a human person is a literary method that is used in the Bible to make spiritual things more easily understood.

We are taken back into time and indeed even before time existed to the beginnings of the process of divine creation of all things. We are in a period called "from everlasting", "before there was an earth", before "the primeval dust" of the world was created by God. This is the start of a new divine initiative that would result in the manifested reality in which we now all live, and which we now all commonly apprehend. This is the building work of God and we are allowed to look in and view the divine builder in the activity of a building sequence.

The first chapter of Genesis has to do with the actual appearance of physical matter caused by the divine speaking forth – "Then God said ...". The earth, the waters, the sun and moon, the planetary system, trees, birds, fish and all living things spring forth at the voice of God. Man is made by the shaping of dust by the actual hand of God and He breathes into man the breath of life.

But the account in *Proverbs Chapter 8* allows us to enter and view the process even before God began to actually speak matter into existence. This is the design phase of the building process – here intent becomes strategic plan and desire is hammered into design; that which has always been in the divine mind becomes grand blueprints or 'technical drawings' on the face of the heavens. These are the blueprints of God – the actual start of the divine initiative; the most accurate expression of the hidden plan held in the heart of God.

Even before God created the actual planets and the earth He had drawn a "circle upon the face of the deep"; assigned limits to the seas that circumscribed how far the waves could advance on the shore; and marked out the foundations of the earth – the hidden substructure upon which the physical earth would securely rest and be stable. This is absolutely amazing stuff!

Everything about God is accurate. There is absolute exactness in His building process. Everything that He builds and manifests is exactly according to the divine blueprints or the divine plan. Since the days of Moses, God insisted that anything that was built to represent His name must be built according to the exactness of the pattern that was seen on the mountain of God by Moses – *Exodus 25:9; 26:40; Numbers 8:4: Acts 7:44*. This is the very nature of God.

Wisdom, this abstract spiritual resource personified here as a speaking woman, declares: *"Then I was beside Him as a master craftsman"*. Here in the deepest dimension of the creative mind of God is the link between the release of wisdom and the building process as indicated in the access to the blueprints of designs of what will become all of the created world. The key declaration of spiritual reality that we come out of this amazing experience with is this: **WISDOM KNOWS THE BLUEPRINTS OR THE INNER DESIGNS OF GOD'S ACCURATE BUILDING.**

This is the resource of the Spirit that was released upon Moses that allowed him to craft an accurate Tabernacle in the Wilderness. This is what came upon David to construct a powerful and even more accurate representation of the mind of God in his day in the Tabernacle of David. This is the resource that was released upon Paul and the early apostles, and this is the dimension that is returning with power upon today's apostles in the 21st century church as final structures, mentalities, truths and understandings are being put in place so that we can push forward to the finish of His purposes in the earth. It is the grace of the master craftsman or what Paul called the master-builder, the '*sophos architekton*' in *1 Corinthians 3:10*.

The word '*architekton*' is the Greek word which provides the root for our English word 'architect'. Much of the meaning has been retained with some exception. In the ancient days the '*architekton*' was a worker on the building site laboring alongside the other builders digging trenches and laying the stones. He was not the high-priced executive that he has become today – he was a worker alongside the common laborers. However, there was one important qualification. While the other workmen labored without knowledge of the final appearance of the structure and had no knowledge how what part of the building they worked on would relate to the finished product, the '*architekton*' would have knowledge of the appearance of the finished building and could direct the work more accurately. He could understand the relationships of the parts of the building to the completed whole. This is the builder's anointing – the grace which rests upon the master craftsmen of the Church.

We have often asked ourselves – "How could Martin Luther be so bold to declare the entire medieval Roman Catholic church to be incorrect and inaccurate in his day?"; "What motivated this Catholic monk to go forward to condemn and destroy the life-structures of his time?" The clear answer is that he saw in the Spirit the accurate structures of God for his day and what was being built did not line up with the blueprint. The building was inaccurate so it had to be torn down. He identified 95 areas of inaccuracy and nailed a listing of them up on the doors of the cathedral at Wittenburg, Germany. His objections are still known as the Ninety-Five Theses of Martin Luther. Though he was never addressed by this title in the darkness of his day Martin Luther, the passionate Catholic monk, was an apostle of God and the grace of the master craftsman or master builder rested upon him.

Today in the Apostolic Reformation move of God, again we find ourselves in the midst of a self-indulgent, materialistic, oppressive and exploiting church, and the apostles that are being accurately raised up by the Spirit of God are registering their objections to the inaccuracy; and expressing through their teaching, doctrine, church-building and the patterns of their personal lives and public ministries the new and more precise shapes of the church that is preferred by God. As they build, God is building through them. He is a building God and His divine intent is to have an accurate Church expressing His nature and Glory in the earth.

This incredible grace of Christ Himself expressing forth through the life of the apostle is given to "perfect" the Church. We must never forget that fact. This sacred deposit is not to be utilized to build personal kingdoms or spiritual empires. It is not released by God to raise up wealth-focused ministries or to be corrupted by defilement from the carnal heart of man. It was released as a dimension of Christ Himself through the lives of selected humans called to be apostles of the Lord commissioned to raise up and bring the saints to full development and perfection for the work of the ministry and the edification of the Body of Christ. Through this awesome medium of the release of the wisdom to build the Church of Jesus Christ will come to full form, manifestation and divine beauty in the earth.

II
Establishing Government

The Old Testament is filled with 'types' of truth that is presented in full operation and function in the New Testament. Paul described the apostolic grace that came upon his life as that which made him a "wise master-builder" (*1 Corinthians 3: 10*). In the Old Testament the person of Solomon is presented as a 'type' or representation of the apostolic grace. He is significant in his wisdom and he built the great Temple (the house of God). Solomon's Temple was the highest order of perfected building of an external structure that had capacity to capture and express the very Presence of God in the earth. After this level God would seek to move to the ultimate order of the expression of His house – the redeemed and sanctified human heart:

> *Do you not know that you are the temple of God and that the Spirit of God dwells in you?*
>
> *1 Corinthians 3: 16 NKJ*

Thus we can see in Solomon many principles for apostolic functionality, apostolic characteristics and apostolic building just as we can see in David a 'type' of many functionalities and characteristics of Kingdom life and operations.

Here we are deep into the process of building the Temple and now Solomon organizes the community to bring back the Ark of God to be installed in its place in the Temple:

> [2] *Now Solomon assembled the elders of Israel and all the heads of the tribes, the chief fathers of the children of Israel, in Jerusalem, that they might bring the ark of the covenant of the LORD up from the City of David, which is Zion.*
>
> [10] *Nothing was in the ark except the two tablets which Moses put there at Horeb, when the LORD made a covenant with the children of Israel, when they had come out of Egypt.*
>
> *2 Chronicles 5: 2 & 10 NKJ*

"Nothing was in the Ark except the two tablets ..." This is a statement of major spiritual significance in understanding the functionality and capability of the apostolic grace and the benefit it brings to the Body of Christ.

It was Moses who built the original Ark by direct instruction of God in his migration out of Egypt. The Book of Hebrews gives information about what Moses the original architect placed inside the Ark:

> ¹ *Then indeed, even the first covenant had ordinances of divine service and the earthly sanctuary.*
>
> ² *For a tabernacle was prepared: the first part, in which was the lampstand, the table, and the showbread, which is called the sanctuary;*
>
> ³ *and behind the second veil, the part of the tabernacle which is called the Holiest of All,*
>
> ⁴ *which had the golden censer and the ark of the covenant overlaid on all sides with gold, in which were the golden pot that had the manna, Aaron's rod that budded, and the tablets of the covenant …*
>
> **Hebrews 9: 1 – 4 NKJ**

Moses placed three objects in the Ark – the tablets of the Law; the pot of manna; the section of Aaron's budding rod. But by the time Solomon installs the Ark in his Temple two of the objects have been removed. We do not know how they were removed but we do know that there were severe consequences in opening the Ark if not totally and completely authorized by God:

> ¹⁹ *But God struck down some of the men of Beth Shemesh, putting seventy of them to death because they had looked into the ark of the LORD. The people mourned because of the heavy blow the LORD had dealt them,*

---

²⁰ *and the men of Beth Shemesh asked, "Who can stand in the presence of the LORD, this holy God? To whom will the ark go up from here?"*

1 Samuel 6: 19 – 20 NIV

We have to assume that two of the objects were either supernaturally removed or directly authorized to be removed from the Ark because they were inconsistent with the apostolic standards that Solomon's Temple were meant to represent. Each of the objects has a particular significance because they were placed in the Ark in a particular context. Let us look at each of them in turn.

The Pot of Manna:

Exodus 16: 1 – 4 NIV

¹ *The whole Israelite community set out from Elim and came to the Desert of Sin, which is between Elim and Sinai, on the fifteenth day of the second month after they had come out of Egypt.*

² *In the desert the whole community grumbled against Moses and Aaron.*

³ *The Israelites said to them, "If only we had died by the LORD's hand in Egypt! There we sat around pots of meat and ate all the food we wanted, but you have brought us out into this desert to starve this entire assembly to death."*

⁴ *Then the LORD said to Moses, "I will rain down bread from heaven for you. The people are to go out each day and gather enough for that day. In this way I will test them and see whether they will follow my instructions."*

Exodus 16: 32 - 34 NIV

[32] *Moses said, "This is what the LORD has commanded: 'Take an omer of manna and keep it for the generations to come, so they can see the bread I gave you to eat in the desert when I brought you out of Egypt.'"*

[33] *So Moses said to Aaron, "Take a jar and put an omer of manna in it. Then place it before the LORD to be kept for the generations to come."*

[34] *As the LORD commanded Moses, Aaron put the manna in front of the Testimony, that it might be kept.*

This was the context in which Manna was placed by the instruction of God into the Ark of the Covenant. The people of God grumbled and revolted against the supply from heaven and against the leaders put in place by God. They lusted for the inferior things of the past and rejected the spiritual migration to a new day in God. The Manna was sent in their rebellion to test them to see if they could follow God completely. God instructed that a pot of Manna be placed in the Ark as a testimony and reminder of their rebellion in the Wilderness.

By the time of Solomon, the pot of Manna in the Ark had been removed - a clear indication of the purification of the attitude and mentality of the people that was represented by the apostolic power of Solomon's beautiful Temple. What a wonderful and hopeful graphical picture of the desire of God for a people that would completely follow him in the modern apostolic day!

Aaron's Rod

Here again we have another picture of the rebellion of the ancient Israelis in the Wilderness:

1 The LORD said to Moses,

2 "Speak to the Israelites and get twelve staffs from them, one from the leader of each of their ancestral tribes. Write the name of each man on his staff.

3 On the staff of Levi write Aaron's name, for there must be one staff for the head of each ancestral tribe.

4 Place them in the Tent of Meeting in front of the Testimony, where I meet with you.

5 The staff belonging to the man I choose will sprout, and I will rid myself of this constant grumbling against you by the Israelites."

6 So Moses spoke to the Israelites, and their leaders gave him twelve staffs, one for the leader of each of their ancestral tribes, and Aaron's staff was among them.

7 Moses placed the staffs before the LORD in the Tent of the Testimony.

8 The next day Moses entered the Tent of the Testimony and saw that Aaron's staff, which represented the house of Levi, had not only sprouted but had budded, blossomed and produced almonds.

9 Then Moses brought out all the staffs from the LORD's presence to all the Israelites. They looked at them, and each man took his own staff.

10 The LORD said to Moses, "Put back Aaron's staff in front of the Testimony, to be kept as a sign to the rebellious. This will put an end to their grumbling against me, so that they will not die."

Numbers 17: 1 – 10 NIV

The placing of the budding Rod before the Lord was as a sign to the rebellious. God wanted to put an end to their grumbling and rebellion against him and his leaders Moses and Aaron. As with the pot of Manna the general context is God's determination to cleanse the people from the carnality of competitiveness; grumbling and discontent; looking backward to a past which was insufficient; revolt against the order of divinely placed leadership and refusal to joyfully migrate onward with God when the spiritual Cloud moved them from one place to another. They hated the Wilderness and all that it brought into their lives. Some of the new things were not comfortable but were necessary to enable the corporate migration onward to the Land of Promise in which the prophetic promises to Abraham would be fulfilled.

Yet in Solomon's order they are all removed indicating that in the realm of the apostolic, the divine order and government of God are affirmed among his people. Only the tablets of the Law remain in the Ark. God is indicating that in the modern apostolic era there is a celebration of obedience and willingness to go forward with God. Deep inside the representation of the Presence of God (the Ark) there is no manifestation of rebellion, disobedience or disrespect. At the core of the present-day apostolic grace and anointing that is brought to the Church there is only a purified heart position to go all the way with God and a willingness to be obedient to His instructions.

The Tablets of the Law represented the government of God within the individual hearts of his people and also within the corporate structure of their community. With an internally governed people - or we may say - with an apostolic people, God could go forth in them and smite the unlawful tribes that occupied the land of Canaan. The guarding of this internal position to keep the law of God in their hearts would be the core of their strength to bring the government of God into the affairs of the nations they were sent to dispossess. The principle was that strong internal law and government assured them of strong externally expressed law and government. The application of this to the modern apostolic era cannot be missed:

> [1] *Hear now, O Israel, the decrees and laws I am about to teach you. Follow them so that you may live and may go in and take possession of the land that the LORD, the God of your fathers, is giving you ...*
>
> [5] *See, I have taught you decrees and laws as the LORD my God commanded me, so that you may follow them in the land you are entering to take possession of it.*
>
> [6] *Observe them carefully, for this will show your wisdom and understanding to the nations, who will hear about all these decrees and say, "Surely this great nation is a wise and understanding people."*
>
> **Deuteronomy 4: 1 & 5-6 NIV**

With the apostolic grace reconfiguring the hearts of the believers and restructuring the internal order of the organized Church in the earth, the government of God is increasingly being openly expressed in the systems of the earth. We may define 'government' this way:

Government is the power flowing from an apostolic church to bring divine regulation and divine impact upon human and satanic systems in the earth to cause the eternal purposes of God to proceed to the Finish in the earth according to Divine plan.

The indispensable Kingdom principle is present here – that there is a vital connection between the state of the heart and the quality and power of outer actions; between the principle that works internally and the accuracy of the action expressed externally. God's government and ability to cause His purposes to move in a straight line to the Finish despite satanic and human opposition is linked to His capacity to govern in the hearts and lives of the Church, His Embassy to the earth.

As long as the "tablets of the Law" remained anchored in the Ark at the core of His Presence, His Kingdom Nation (the Church) would prevail against all His enemies and bring His dominance and ruler-ship to visibility in the systems of the earth and in the hearts of men.

FIVE

DIMENSIONS OF
THE APOSTOLIC
The Building Power of the Cyrus Anointing

W e have already seen that the apostolic is deeply
connected to the building grace that comes from the
Lord. Paul described the grace that fell upon his life as the grace
that made him a "wise master-builder" (*1 Corinthians 3:10*); and
he speaks of this in the context of a vast and general building
activity of moving the Church to a place of maturity and
perfection.

Patterns in Cyrus the Builder of the House of God

Let us now look at Cyrus who was used in the Word as a
powerful image, representation or 'type' of the building grace
of the apostolic. He in fact initiated a massive and significant

building movement and restoration of the Temple or House of God at Jerusalem:

> *¹ In the first year of Cyrus king of Persia, in order to fulfill the word of the LORD spoken by Jeremiah, the LORD moved the heart of Cyrus king of Persia to make a proclamation throughout his realm and also to put it in writing:*
>
> *² "This is what Cyrus king of Persia says: 'The LORD, the God of heaven, has given me all the kingdoms of the earth and he has appointed me to build a temple for him at Jerusalem in Judah*
>
> *³ Any of his people among you may go up to Jerusalem in Judah and build the temple of the LORD, the God of Israel, the God who is in Jerusalem, and may their God be with them.*
>
> *⁴ And in any locality where survivors may now be living, the people are to provide them with silver and gold, with goods and livestock, and with freewill offerings for the temple of God in Jerusalem.'"*

Ezra 1: 1 – 42 NIV

Cyrus is the fulfillment of the prophetic utterance of Jeremiah who prophesied a return and restoration of life in Jerusalem after the years of devastation and exile caused by the invasion of the Babylonians. Now the time has come for fulfillment and the reality of fulfillment manifests in the life of Cyrus. Thus we can say that the apostolic proclamation and activity brings prophetic fulfillment and divine validation!

Cyrus issues a proclamation – a declaration in the earth of a divine and heavenly decision. It causes systems and times to radically shift and change and it heralds the beginning of a new divine movement among God's people. All of these are patterns of the power of apostolic activity.

There are Four Components of the Cyrus (Apostolic) Mandate.

1. **The Issue of Government and Dominion**
   "The LORD, the God of heaven, has given me all the kingdoms of the earth"

   Ezra 1: 2

Nothing in the authority of Cyrus starts within himself. The genesis of his power is with God and so it is with the genuine apostolic grace. Cyrus says: "The Lord God of Heaven has given me all the kingdoms of the earth." He is a ruler who sits upon a throne and he does exercise power and strength in the earth but here he indicates the true source of his manifested strength – it is not from him but from the God of Heaven. In his statement is the reality of core humility and death to self that is a fundamental feature of the apostolic.

2. **The Identification of the Command to Build**
   "...and he has appointed me to build a temple for him at Jerusalem in Judah"

   Ezra 1: 2

The original Hebrew language indicates that a strong commission or a command was placed upon the life of Cyrus. There is a recognition that a superior heavenly power has oversight of his life and that superior power has issued a command, an appointment or a commission that cannot be denied. This is the activation point of the apostolic grace that will manifest through Cyrus.

The activity of building always has the end or the destination in sight. No one starts to build with the intention of not finishing. Building moves always to a definite Finish! Building is filled with strategic intent and requires a determined but forward-looking mentality:

> ²⁸ *"Suppose one of you wants to build a tower. Won't you first sit down and estimate the cost to see if you have enough money to complete it?*
>
> ²⁹ *For if you lay the foundation and are not able to finish it, everyone who sees it will ridicule you,*
>
> ³⁰ *saying, 'This person began to build and wasn't able to finish.'..."*
>
> **Luke 14: 28 – 30 NIV**

Jesus Himself in revealing to us His mission in the Church indicates this as His core intent in *Matthew 16: 18*: *"... on this rock I will build my church, and the gates of Hades will not overcome it. "*

3. *The Release of Empowerment and Activation*
    to the People
    "Any of his people ... may go up to Jerusalem in Judah and build the temple"

    Ezra 1: 3

With the declaration of a new era of building comes the massive empowerment of the people. The proclamation of Cyrus carries within it what we call **The Equalization Factor**. "Any" of his people may go up to Jerusalem and build. He empowers everybody! And in doing so he redefines the mentality of the people. There is no one who is weak and incapable! The decree of Cyrus assumes that all have the capability and the capacity to contribute to the building of the house of God. This is widespread and comprehensive empowerment of ALL the saints and this is an essential component of the true apostolic paradigm sweeping through the Body of Christ today.

The apostolic has brought an Era of Empowerment - the removal of the mentalities of weakness and insufficiency that have shrouded the minds of the saints and caused the release of divinely-birthed confidence in the hearts of God's people that they have the right, the authority and the mandate to begin to move their lives towards final spiritual development and maturity.

We remind ourselves of the fundamental description of the apostolic as part of the five functions released by the ascended Christ:

> 11 *So Christ himself gave the apostles, the prophets, the evangelists, the pastors and teachers,*
>
> 12 *to equip his people for works of service, so that the body of Christ may be built up*
>
> 13 *until we all reach unity in the faith and in the knowledge of the Son of God and become mature, attaining to the whole measure of the fullness of Christ.*
>
> **Ephesians 4: 11 - 13 NIV**

In this apostolic day the saints are to be made strong and responsible and empowered to participate in the powerful movement of the Church to maturity and to the end of Time!

4. **The Provision of Resources and the Destruction of the Spirit of Lack**

And in any locality where survivors may now be living, the people are to provide them with silver and gold, with goods and livestock, and with freewill offerings for the temple of God in Jerusalem.

Ezra 1: 4

Cyrus commanded that the people returning to build the Temple should be supplied generously with whatever they needed to do the work - whether it was gold or goods or livestock.

In the great building effort of the Church today, as the structure of the Body of Christ is being brought by the Spirit of God to a state of completion, the greatest requirement of the people for accurate building is the supply of the Word of God. It is a day of revelation as the apostles of the church today break open the meaning and application of the word of God into the hearts of the saints.

The emphasis has shifted towards accuracy. The word is not being preached to entertain or to simply excite the emotions of the saints. This is completely irrelevant activity in a season when a building command has gone forth from heaven. The word is being released to make the saints competent to live accurately, to walk powerfully in the actual will of God and to build their personal and community lives in exact accordance with the requirements from Heaven.

It is a building day – a day in which the word of God is being translated into powerful and accurate lifestyle in the earth!

The Apostolic Core of the Cyrus Activity

Isaiah 44: 26 – 28 NIV

26 *(The Lord) … who carries out the words of his servants and fulfills the predictions of his messengers, who says of Jerusalem, 'It shall be inhabited,' of the towns of Judah, 'They shall be rebuilt,' and of their ruins, 'I will restore them,'*
27 *who says to the watery deep, 'Be dry, and I will dry up your streams,'*
28 *who says of Cyrus, 'He is my shepherd and will accomplish all that I please; he will say of Jerusalem, "Let it be rebuilt," and of the temple, "Let its foundations be laid."*

Isaiah is prophesying 100 years before the birth of Cyrus the king of Persia and he calls him by his actual future name. The context into which he is speaking is the restoration of the nation from a state of spiritual wreckage and departure from God and the declaration of a new season in the Lord.

Cyrus here is used as a powerful representation of the building dimension of the apostolic and we can identify several features of this in Cyrus.

In verse 26 Isaiah describes the activity of the Lord:
… who carries out the words of his servants and fulfills the predictions of his messengers, who says of Jerusalem, 'It shall

*be inhabited,' of the towns of Judah, 'They shall be rebuilt''
and of their ruins, 'I will restore them,'...*

Isaiah 44: 26

The words describe what is in the heart of God. The towns of
Judah and the community life in them shall be rebuilt and all
the ruins will be restored. Later in verse 28 Isaiah describes the
proclamation that comes forth from Cyrus and he becomes a
clear reflection of the heart of God: *"he will say of Jerusalem, "Let
it be rebuilt," and of the temple, "Let its foundations be laid."* The
words of Cyrus and the heart of God are one and the same! This
is a clear indicator of how the position and teaching of the
apostle synchronizes completely with the heart and desire of
God.

Cyrus is a shepherd of the people and that carries an
understanding of his role to gather, protect and nurture the
people of God. He will accomplish everything that God pleases,
thus he has an emphasis on execution, application and actual
doing not just empty proclamation. This is consistent with the
building emphasis that the apostolic brings to the Church.

The apostolic shifts the emphasis in the Body of Christ from
simply blessing people to make them feel good in the conduct
of a good church service to an emphasis on discovering and
implementing the will and purpose of the Lord at the time.

The thing that is commended by the Lord when we come before
Him at the end of time is not just how we felt in our salvation

but how well we executed the will and purpose of the Lord. Jesus in presenting the Kingdom of Heaven says:

> His lord said to him, *'Well done, good and faithful servant; you have been faithful over a few things, I will make you ruler over many things. Enter into the joy of your lord.'*
>
> **Matthew 25: 23 NIV**

The core of the apostolic is the accomplishment of things in the Spirit. The grace of the apostolic restores to individuals, families and communities the practical spiritual power and competence to actually discover and implement the will of God for their lives on every level. Thus full maturity becomes very functional and very practical indeed.

Aspects of the Apostolic Anointing

> *Isaiah 45: 1 - 6 NKJ*
> [1] *"Thus says the LORD to His anointed, To Cyrus, whose right hand I have held — To subdue nations before him And loose the armor of kings, To open before him the double doors, So that the gates will not be shut:*
> [2] *'I will go before you and make the crooked places straight; I will break in pieces the gates of bronze and cut the bars of iron.*
> [3] *I will give you the treasures of darkness and hidden riches of secret places, that you may know that I, the LORD, who call you by your name, am the God of Israel.*
> [4] *For Jacob My servant's sake, And Israel My elect, I have even called you by your name; I have named you, though you have not known Me.*

⁵ I am the LORD, and there is no other; there is no God besides Me. I will gird you, though you have not known Me, ⁶that they may know from the rising of the sun to its setting that there is none besides Me. I am the LORD, and there is no other; …

1. "Whose right hand I have held" – Isaiah 45: 1

The word used in Hebrew translated as "held" is *'Chazaq'*: *to strengthen, to prevail, to be resolute, to be firm, to be courageous.* The right hand represents ability and authority; the power to accomplish and to do. This is the strength of the apostolic and it comes directly from God and not from the human personality, training or determination.

¹³ For I hold you by your right hand – I, the LORD your God. And I say to you, 'Don't be afraid. I am here to help you.
¹⁴ Though you are a lowly worm, O Jacob, don't be afraid, people of Israel, for I will help you. I am the LORD, your Redeemer. I am the Holy One of Israel.'
¹⁵ You will be a new threshing instrument with many sharp teeth. You will tear your enemies apart, making chaff of mountains.
¹⁶ You will toss them into the air, and the wind will blow them all away; a whirlwind will scatter them. Then you will rejoice in the LORD. You will glory in the Holy One of Israel.
Isaiah 41: 13 – 16 NLT

When God takes hold of your right hand or it could be said - when the Lord imparts His strength and comes alongside you in the mission then fear departs. Fear is the result of intimidation. Though we are a "worm" and really have very little personal strength and power, we are able to press forward and not be intimidated by the power of the darkness around us. The release of the apostolic anointing into the Church creates a bold Church that moves forward without fear. This is an important factor in the days in which we live when the surrounding darkness is becoming thicker and the hearts of men have plunged into disobedience and rebellion against God.

The presence of God coming alongside is a transforming power. God makes the "worm" Jacob into a "threshing instrument with many sharp teeth" that can destroy the mountains and the hills. Transformation produces functionality and accurate productivity. Suddenly the context is one of battle, victory and overwhelming strength against the enemy. The partnership of the Holy Spirit in the battle is very clear. "You will toss them into the air" but "the wind will blow them all away". The Holy Spirit is the "wind" that works alongside the critically important efforts of man to complete what man has started. We are describing features of the apostolic environment.

2.   *"To subdue nations and loose the armor of kings"* –
     Isaiah 45: 1
The context of the Church today is that we are moving forward towards the End of Time. The Finish of all things is close and the systems of the earth are breaking down just as the prophets have prophesied. The hearts of men are filled with fear and the "wise men" of the earth have no answers to the vexing problems of the day. Crisis upon crisis is breaking upon the nations of the earth and the cry of despair is increasing. But within the Body of Christ there is arising hope, faith, joy, maturity and high expectation that the journey through Time is almost over and our Home in eternity is very near! These two

conditions – despair in the hearts of the unbelievers and hope in the hearts of the redeemed – have been prophesied by the ancients:

> ¹ *"Arise, Jerusalem! Let your light shine for all to see. For the glory of the LORD rises to shine on you.*
> ² *Darkness as black as night covers all the nations of the earth, but the glory of the LORD rises and appears over you.*
> ³ *All nations will come to your light; mighty kings will come to see your radiance. "*
>
> **Isaiah 60: 1 – 3   NLT**

The crisis of the day is an opportunity for impact - *"The nations will come to your light!"* God will subdue nations before the Cyrus People *(Isaiah 45:1)*. The reference to nations speaks of the vastness of the scale of the divine movement. The apostolic anointing in the midst of the Church imparts to the Body of Christ the capacity to move with God on a larger scale than we have ever moved before. The mission and purposes of God being released through the apostolic grace are not just limited to individual churches and communities but to the vastness of the planet as a whole.

Apostolic community spread across nations and continents are synchronized into one-ness and agreement by focused apostolic vision. In defiance of the fragmentation and brokenness of the earth the people of God are speaking with one voice, and hearing the same thing with great inner joy and agreement. A sight of the holistic plan of God is falling into the earth.

Through the strength of the global apostolic anointing God has released a Day of Divine Battle. Dark powers in the heavenly places – kings and principalities – are being stripped of their powers as the Body of Christ in the earth rises into powerful Governmental Prayer across the nations. The words of Paul are resounding with startling clarity in the day in which we live:

> 12 *For we are not fighting against flesh-and-blood enemies, but against evil rulers and authorities of the unseen world, against mighty powers in this dark world, and against evil spirits in the heavenly places.*
>
> 13 *Therefore, put on every piece of God's armor so you will be able to resist the enemy in the time of evil. Then after the battle you will still be standing firm.*
>
> **Ephesians 6: 12 – 13 NLT**

The saints have been empowered and now believe that they can rise in powerful spiritual battle against the enemies of God to take control of the realms of the spirit to cause the final purposes of the Lord to come swiftly into the earth. The prophetic words of Jeremiah are being fulfilled in the apostolic day in which we live:

> 30 *"… Babylon's warriors have stopped fighting; they remain in their strongholds. Their strength is exhausted; they have become weaklings. Her dwellings are set on fire; the bars of her gates are broken.*
>
> 31 *One courier follows another and messenger follows messenger to announce to the king of Babylon that his entire city is captured,*
>
> 32 *the river crossings seized, the marshes set on fire, and the soldiers terrified."*
>
> **Jeremiah 51: 30 – 32 NIV**

3. *"To open the double doors that the gates be not shut"* –
   Isaiah 45: 1

The double doors are a reference to the two-paneled doors that
formed the entrance to the Holy Place in the Temple seen by
Ezekiel in the vision of the heavens.

> 23 *Both the main hall and the Most Holy Place had double*
> *doors.*
> 24 *Each door had two leaves--two hinged leaves for each door.*
>
> *Ezekiel 41: 23 – 24 NIV*

Thus the double doors represent access to the Presence of God.
God Himself will open the double doors unto Cyrus. He will
grant him not just the personal anointing upon his life but also
the partnership of the very Presence of God as he goes forth into
the divine mission. Keep in mind that we are looking into the
mind of God and detailing the features of the apostolic reality.

The leadership and companionship of the Presence of God is a
vital component of the spiritual journey and necessary for
accuracy and success. Clear revelation of the importance of this
was provided us in the days of Moses:

> 13 *"… If you are pleased with me, teach me your ways so I may*
> *know you and continue to find favor with you. Remember that*
> *this nation is your people."*
> 14 *The LORD replied, "My Presence will go with you, and I*
> *will give you rest."*
> 15 *Then Moses said to him, "If your Presence does not go with*
> *us, do not send us up from here.*
> 16 *How will anyone know that you are pleased with me and*

with your people unless you go with us? What else will distinguish me and your people from all the other people on the face of the earth? ..."

Exodus 33: 13 – 16 NIV

Here the Presence of God gave the people "rest" in the midst of the spiritual labor and journey. It is vital to the sending. *"If your Presence does not go with us, do not send us up from here."* It became an indicator to all the world that God was pleased with his people and it would distinguish them as different from all the other people on the face of the earth.

In promising to Cyrus that He would open to him the double doors God is declaring all of these realities to an apostolic people.

When the double doors are opened "the gates will not be shut". All systems that shut the hearts of men to the word of the Lord will be broken. The enemy will not have the power to close off against the on-coming apostolic advance. The systems of human organization in the earth will be open to invasion by the power of the Kingdom of God. No gates will be shut because the very Presence of God is moving with His people. This is describing an atmosphere of victory in the earth and the inability of the Darkness to prevent the overwhelming spread of the divine mission. We are describing the environment of a global apostolic movement in the earth and we can see in that description the nature of the Church that must be in the earth in the Last Days.

4. *"Make crooked places straight; break the gates of bronze; cut the bars of iron" - Isaiah 45: 2*
The NIV Translation says: *"I will go before you and level the mountains"*. The original word used in the Hebrew is *'yashar'* – justice, straight, level or a reference to ethical uprightness. This is the environment of the Cyrus anointing. When God goes before us the requirement is for ethical correctness, righteousness and clear and accurate application of the principles of the Kingdom of God.

The true apostolic is directly connected to the proclamation of correct life. Within the environs of the apostolic grace there must be an emphasis on the movement of individual and community life to fit what the Word of God has said. The apostolic follows God into the mission in God's ways, not the ways of tradition or the corrupt ways of the world system. The apostolic is linked to purity and correct structures of life and this must be clearly seen and heard in the proclamation of the apostles of the Body of Christ.

When the ways of the apostolic are aligned with the ways of God then the "gates of bronze" are broken and the "bars of iron" are cut. These are clear references to the resistance and opposition of the satanic systems in the earth and in the hearts and minds of men. Breakthrough occurs as we surge forward deep within the divine principles. The release of the apostolic grace fills the Church not just with the power of correctness and ethical purity but also with great divine momentum and unstoppable advance!

5.　*"I will give the treasures of darkness and hidden riches of secret places" – Isaiah 45: 3*

The Berkeley Translation says: *"Hoarded wealth of secret places."* God Himself will supply the resources necessary for the advancement of the mission in an apostolic environment. This suggests a faith that is not consistent with the natural supply systems of the earth realm. As the Church moves forward towards the End, God Himself will supply the necessary material resources in defiance to the limitations and restrictions of the earth realm. God's people will not be left without supply and resource.

When Moses departed Egypt leading the people of God into the wilderness on a long journey to the Promised Land they were loaded down with the material resources of the Egyptian system. This was according to the command of God to Moses:

> 35 *The Israelites did as Moses instructed and asked the Egyptians for articles of silver and gold and for clothing.*
> 36 *The LORD had made the Egyptians favorably disposed toward the people, and they gave them what they asked for; so they plundered the Egyptians.*
>
> *Exodus 12: 35 – 36　NIV*

Divine supply of all necessary natural and material resources is an integral part of the Cyrus apostolic context. The prophets have prophesied of the certainty of supply of resource as the Church moves forcefully towards the end of Time led by powerful apostolic functionality:

> 3 *Nations will come to your light, and kings to the brightness of your dawn.*

---

⁴ *"Lift up your eyes and look about you: All assemble and come to you; your sons come from afar, and your daughters are carried on the hip.*

⁵ *Then you will look and be radiant, your heart will throb and swell with joy; the wealth on the seas will be brought to you, to you the riches of the nations will come.*

⁶ *Herds of camels will cover your land, young camels of Midian and Ephah. And all from Sheba will come, bearing gold and incense and proclaiming the praise of the LORD. ... "*

Isaiah 60: 3 - 6 NIV

The Word of God provides the framework for the structure and the expression of our faith. In an apostolic day we are rising to new faith levels and believing God for the full manifestation of all of His word to us.

6. *"I have called you by your name; I have named you"* - *Isaiah 45: 4*

The issues here have to do with strong identity granted by the Lord to saints moving forward in an apostolic environment. To be named by the Lord suggests that we now take our identity within what the Lord is doing at the time. He has broken us free from the false "naming" of the earth realm and the incorrect identities forced upon His Body by cultures, nations, philosophies and the things of the earth. We are being prepared for life in another realm which is eternal and immortal.

He is calling us by our name! The instructions and the directions of the Lord guiding the apostolic people forward in this day are coming on the frequency of our new identity in

Him. As we are transformed by the power of the apostolic anointing into what God wants us to be we are able to receive clear, direct instructions from heaven that will send us forward into the divine purpose. This is true for individuals, families and communities. God has named us! Identity is linked to knowledge and prophetic hearing. Truly the sheep now hear the voice and commands of the Shepherd!

In the end the Cyrus anointing causes a global, earth-shaking revelation of God. *"That they may know from the rising to the setting of the sun, people may know there is none besides me. I am the LORD, and there is no other:"* that is, from end to end of the earth.

Of great comfort to the apostolic saints in the earth today is that the ways of Cyrus will be directed by the Lord:
> *I have raised him up in righteousness, And I will direct all his ways; He shall build My city and let My exiles go free, not for price nor reward," says the LORD of hosts.*
>
> **Isaiah 45:13 NKJ**

In closing, the apostolic reality for the Body of Christ that is patterned in the commission given by God to Cyrus provides us with a powerful listing of benefits that are given by God to His Church in these last days provided through the release of the apostolic grace to the Body.

The Cyrus Apostolic Resource

- God will hold his right hand and empower him with courage and momentum;

- Nations are subdued and vast divine purpose is released;
- Satanic kings and princes of the heaven are stripped of their defenses;
- Access is given to heavenly places in God to bring forth divine purpose;
- Crooked places are straightened; mountains leveled; and a correct ethical environment is created for us to move forward in;
- Material resources are provided from hidden heavenly storehouses;
- New identity is granted as God calls us by name and we receive enhanced empowerment in Christ;
- God directs our ways in righteousness and building power is released to us.

SIX

APOSTOLIC FATHERING
AND MENTORING

Read: 2 Timothy 2: 1 – 2

*T*here is important reproductive activity taking place here
– the transference of the apostolic seed from generation
to generation. Generational transference is an important
activity. Finishing is an essential component of the apostolic
grace and there is no way that we can arrive at the final
conclusion of the purposes of God in the earth, unless we
master the spiritual ability to move the gains of a former
generation entirely to the next without loss of definition, quality
or power.

The issue of powerful communication to the next generation is
of great importance to God:

> *30 A posterity shall serve Him. It will be recounted of the Lord
> to the next generation,*

³¹ *They will come and declare His righteousness to a people who will be born, that He has done this.*

Psalm 22: 30 - 31 NKJ

⁴ *We will not hide them from their children, telling to the generation to come the praises of the LORD, and His strength and His wonderful works that He has done.*
⁵ *For He established a testimony in Jacob, and appointed a law in Israel, which He commanded our fathers, that they should make them known to their children;*
⁶ *That the generation to come might know them, the children who would be born, that they may arise and declare them to their children,*
⁷ *That they may set their hope in God, <u>and not forget</u> the works of God, but keep His commandments.*

Psalm 78: 4 - 7 NKJ

One generation shall praise Your works to another and shall declare Your mighty acts.

Psalm 145: 4

The key issue here is that the next generation must not "forget" the works of the Lord. The word *"forget"* also means "to wither" and refers to a drying up or a withering of the dimension of God built by the previous generation of power. Apostolic generation is ensured by the orderly and strategic transfer of the doctrine to another generation, which has the internal quality to keep the value of the word delivered to it still fresh and strong in the earth.

Malachi closes off the prophetic era of the Old Testament with a blistering word that echoes across the 400 years dividing the Old from the New Covenants:

> 5 *"... Behold, I will send you Elijah the prophet before the coming of the great and dreadful day of the LORD.*
>
> *6 And he will turn the hearts of the fathers to the children, and the hearts of the children to their fathers, lest I come and strike the earth with a curse."*

Malachi 4: 5 – 6

Essential to the finalization of purpose in the earth is the release of an Elijah Dimension which will cause a rejoining of the generations, a turning of the hearts of the fathers to the children and vice versa. This is so important that the earth is cursed if it does not occur. What a powerful statement to indicate a primary desire in the heart of God, that the spirit of abortion that stops the full transference of spiritual value between the generations is destroyed forever!

Here in the message to Timothy, Paul speaks to his spiritual son and urges him to keep the dream alive by transferring the spiritual deposit to sons of his own, men of quality who will ensure that the apostolic value is maintained in purity and power. Essential to an understanding of this powerful process of transference is an examination of the reality of spiritual son-ship in the Word of God.

Spiritual Son-ship and Apostolic Grace

Let us look at four important issues in the relationship of apostolic fathers to their spiritual sons.

Son-ship Principle 1: Equality in Soul
Philippians 2: 19 - 23 NKJ
19 *But I trust in the Lord Jesus to send Timothy to you shortly, that I also may be encouraged when I know your state.*
20 *For I have no one like-minded, who will sincerely care for your state.*
21 *For all seek their own, not the things which are of Christ Jesus.*
22 *But you know his proven character, that as a son with his father he served with me in the gospel.*
23 *Therefore I hope to send him at once, as soon as I see how it goes with me.*

Paul is writing to the Philippian church from prison exhorting them to be "of one accord, of one mind" *(Philippians 2:2)*. The apostolic cry is that there is a shortage of qualified workers who will accurately demonstrate and share his heart with the precious saints at the church in Philippi. Workers are consumed by self-interest and are insincere in their relationships with the church. Their character is defective and they are invalidated as proper representatives of the apostolic order. In the midst of this apparently negative picture stands Timothy, one who serves as a son with his father in the gospel of Jesus Christ.

Timothy is "like-minded" with his apostolic source and mentor. The word is: *'isopsuchos',* literally translated *equal in soul.* The word demonstrates a necessity for a similarity of values between the spiritual father and the son. They must share the same intensity and the same pattern of spiritual values. Both hearts must beat to the same frequency; there must be no difference in their patterns of care or concern. This is required for effective apostolic representation. Both Paul and Timothy have very different personalities in the natural, but share the same heart and the same values in the realm of spiritual ministry. This is essential for accurate apostolic fathering.

Son-ship Principle 2: Legitimate Birthing
Titus 1: 4 – 5 NKJ
> [4] To Titus, _a true son_ in our common faith: Grace, mercy, and peace from God the Father and the Lord Jesus Christ our Savior.
> [5] For this reason I left you in Crete, that you should set in order the things that are lacking, and appoint elders in every city as I commanded you--

Titus is elevated into significant apostolic operations and authority through the receiving of the command of his spiritual father because he is a "true" son. The word here is *'gnesios': a legitimately birthed son*. This word speaks of the genuine and thorough processes that caused Titus to claim the place of legitimate heir of spiritual authority coming forth from the life of Paul.

The issue of a spiritual process is important in the journey to the place of spiritual son-ship. The authority of a son and the grace to receive and to function in the mantle of a father does not come easily or cheaply.
> [5] And you have forgotten the exhortation which speaks to you as to sons: "My son, do not despise the chastening of the Lord, nor be discouraged when you are rebuked by Him;
> [6] For whom the Lord loves He chastens, and scourges every son whom He receives."

> *⁷ If you endure chastening, God deals with you as with sons;*
> *for what son is there whom a father does not chasten?*
> *⁸ But if you are without chastening, of which all have become*
> *partakers, then you are illegitimate and not sons.*
>
> *Hebrews 12: 5 – 8 NKJ*

The general principle established here is that legitimacy comes through the process. This is what one apostle I know calls "development by damage." One who avoids the spiritual process and the development which is caused by the Lord in his life through internal transformation, confrontation of deficiency, acceptance of mentoring, learning of obedience, receiving of rebuke and encouragement, is illegitimate and has no authority to receive and use the authority of his spiritual father.

The process of personal development and mentoring is not always pleasant. The apostolic father may confront many issues in his son's life as he causes spiritual growth and transformation inside of him. The end of the process however is always geared to abundant ministry and productions of apostolic patterns.

> *Now no chastening seems to be joyful for the present, but*
> *painful; nevertheless, afterward it yields the peaceable fruit of*
> *righteousness to those who have been trained by it.*
>
> *Hebrews 12: 11 NKJ*

Son-ship Principle 3: Paternal Impartation
2 Timothy 1: 2 – 6 NKJ
² To Timothy, a beloved son: Grace, mercy, and peace from
God the Father and Christ Jesus our Lord.

³ I thank God, whom I serve with a pure conscience, as my forefathers did, as without ceasing I remember you in my prayers night and day,
⁴ greatly desiring to see you, being mindful of your tears, that I may be filled with joy,
⁵ when I call to remembrance the genuine faith that is in you, which dwelt first in your grandmother Lois and your mother Eunice, and I am persuaded is in you also.
⁶ Therefore I remind you to stir up the gift of God which is in you <u>through the laying on of my hands</u>.

The context of the relationship between Paul and Timothy is clearly highly emotional and intimate. Paul ceaselessly prays for the increase of the high-quality faith that is in Timothy which has been handed down to him from his mother and grandmother. The apostle seeks to increase the dimension that is in Timothy by the laying on of his hands upon him in order to impart to him the "gift of God".

The "gift of God" will cause an acceleration of the spiritual benefit operating in Timothy's life. Paul's ministration to him is a life-enhancer. It causes the potential and the foundational quality that is in Timothy to explode to new dimensions. Timothy can stir up a fresh deposit of the Spirit that has come into him and find new levels of ministry, character, spiritual power and performance that comes to his life through the direct impact of his "father" Paul. Such can be the impact of the hands of the apostolic father in the life of his son.

The impartation that comes in to Timothy transforms his emotional life. He has not received "the spirit of fear but of love, power and soundness of mind" *(verse 7)*. He comes forth more fortified inwardly, more psychologically complete and emotionally strong. The affirmation and clear support and impartation of his apostle have pushed him to a new level of performance and function in Christ.

Son-ship Principle 4: Hearing the father's voice.
2 Timothy 2: 2 NKJ
And the things that you have heard from me among many witnesses ...

The impartation of the spiritual seed from the apostolic father comes by "hearing" and the very meaning of the word carries with it suggestions of intimacy between the one who speaks and the one who hears the spoken voice. This is received utterance in the context of relationship. The same word is used in *John 8: 43*:

"... Why do you not understand My speech? Because you are not able to listen to My word. ..."
John 8: 43 NKJ

Understanding in this context requires a capacity or an ability to hear the word. Those listening to the words of Jesus did not possess this capacity and so they were entirely unable to decode the mystery of His speech. He spoke plainly and they remained darkened. The spiritual son must have developed the capacity to hear the words of the apostolic father on a level much deeper than simply mental understanding of his language. He must be able to decode the patterns of his spiritual father's heart and the thrusts of the Lord's further purpose in his doctrine. How else could he represent the apostle accurately as Timothy was able to do for Paul?

This capacity is developed through enduring the process of transformation that is activated in the heart of the spiritual son through relationship with the apostle and through receiving his teaching and the patterns of his lifestyle. As the capacity to hear grows so too does the ability to accurately transmit the apostolic message.

Father and Son: Elijah and Elisha

The enduring spiritual model of transference through son-ship is the model of Elijah and Elisha. In *1 Kings 19* Elijah is commanded by the Lord to anoint Elisha the son of Shaphat to be prophet after him. Elisha becomes a servant and a spiritual son to Elijah and becomes an active participant in Elijah's spiritual journey. In *2 Kings 2* Elijah comes to the end of his course and releases his mantle to Elisha as he is taken up by the chariots of the Lord.

God has commissioned Elijah with three final tasks – to anoint Jehu as king of Israel, to anoint Hazael as king of Syria and to place Elisha as prophet after him. Elijah completes only two of the assignments, but it is his son Elisha who sends a servant to anoint Jehu as king of Israel to complete the purpose of Elijah long after his departure from the earth.

Elisha enters into the accurate prophetic patterns of Elijah through son-ship even after his departure, and he himself is able to release powerful original prophetic purposes to an unnamed servant who he has in turn fathered. Such is the trans-generational power of apostolic fathering and mentoring.

Who Can Receive the Apostolic Word?

2 Timothy 2: 2 NKJ
And the things that you have heard from me among many witnesses, commit these to faithful men who will be able to teach others also.

The seed of the word that has been received must be transmitted to faithful men. There is a quality component to the further transference of the apostolic word. The word "faithful" contains the emphasis of an active believing and it indicates persons who are reliable, trustworthy and who can keep or hold confidence. This is not a passive condition, but a state of increasing growth in character and ability to honor that which has been received from the apostolic source. What has been received is now being transferred to others of equal internal quality.

Jesus clearly indicated the standards for transfer of spiritual resources:
Do not give what is holy to the dogs; nor cast your pearls before swine, lest they trample them under their feet, and turn and tear you in pieces.
Matthew 7: 6 NKJ

125

What is "holy" or a "pearl" to you must also be holy and a pearl in the hearts and minds of those to whom you give it. If there is an incorrect estimation of the value of the resource received, then there will be inappropriate action taken as a result. You are ministering what has become precious to you – values, attitudes, biblical truth, faith, principles, lifestyle definition, wisdom, doctrine, insights, revelations all transferred through an apostle-father relationship. It is the responsibility of the son to place a high value on what has been received from the father and then to insist on the same quality in the hearts of the sons he raises up so that the value of the apostolic word will continue on to another ministry generation.

These faithful men must be <u>able</u> to teach others also. The word here is not *'dunatos'* or *'ischuros'* which convey the meaning of might or power, but it is the word *'hikanos'* which indicates the possessing of internal capacity, personal sufficiency or ability to reach to a certain level. This ability is the internal capacity of character and spirit to receive the apostolic word. It directly refers to depth of heart, endurance, capacity of believing and thoroughness of spiritual processing within. It is to men of such worth that the value of son-ship and the value of the apostolic word are passed to ensure that the apostolic deposit remains pure and strong in the earth.

The word will be committed to these men. It will be "placed near to them" and made available to them for use and development in their lives. These downstream recipients of the apostolic grace go out to teach "others also". Again, the word used in the original language in which the scripture was written releases much understanding to us.

"Others" is the word *'heteros'*. It indicates others of a different nature or of a different generic distinction. The phrase indicates that men who have received the apostolic impartation go out to teach others of a different nature and persuasion in the same way, and with the same values, with which they have been taught. The impartation received when you were of a different character and order from the apostolic source caused you to be changed into a state similar to the apostolic source. Now you are empowered to go out to find and teach others who will be changed into what you are. Through son-ship and the downstream teaching of the apostolic word and delivery of the apostolic patterns, the integrity of the apostolic source and the reality of his mantle and gifting remain undiminished in the earth. An increasing order of apostolic quality is created and the foundations of the Church continue to be built.

To summarize, several things occur in the midst of the reality of apostolic mentoring and spiritual son-ship:

- There is the creation of a core of ministry of the same nature and character as their apostolic father, developed in the earth by direct personal impartation and teaching.

- The process is developmental and ongoing as sons become fathers and go on to make sons themselves while at the same time keeping the integrity of the apostolic deposit alive in their hearts.

- The entire system involves a growing up into maturity. The necessity to receive spiritual processing and personal transformation cannot be denied. The work of the Holy Spirit in bringing men to maturity and full development is essential to the entire apostolic process.

4 "The Lord GOD has given Me the tongue of the learned, that I should know how to speak a word in season to him who is weary. He awakens Me morning by morning, he awakens My ear to hear as the learned.

5 The Lord GOD has opened My ear; and I was not rebellious, nor did I turn away."

Isaiah 50: 4 – 5 NKJ

SEVEN

APOSTOLIC SPHERES
AND GLOBAL MINISTRY

Read 2 Corinthians Chapters 10 - 11

*T*he core issue that Paul encounters here at the Corinthian church is an incorrect expression of apostolic authority which caused two things:

- the immaturity of the perception of the saints who are able to "see" only the outward appearance of ministry coming to them, and
- the deliberate inaccurate projection of their apostolic measure by the "false" apostles coming into the church.

The result of all this inaccuracy was that the church was incapable of correctly assessing the value of the apostolic ministry brought to them by Paul. Because Paul does not present his personal greatness to the church by emphasis on his outward appearance, the people reject his authority and despise his position in Christ:

> 10 *"For his letters," they say, "are weighty and powerful, but his bodily presence is weak, and his speech contemptible."*
>
> 11 *Let such a person consider this, that what we are in word by letters when we are absent, such we will also be in deed when we are present.*
>
> **2 Corinthians 10: 10 – 11 NKJ**

Paul pleads to the people of Corinth is the "meekness and gentleness of Christ". The apostolic arrival is not in the manifestation of personal power and self-aggrandizement, but in the accuracy of the nature and character of Christ Himself. These principles are being declared powerfully today by the accurate apostles of this Apostolic Reformation as the Spirit of God destroys the false concepts of ministry that have distorted the discernment power of the Church across the earth.

Nowadays the Church cannot even perceive the reality of the apostolic measure except it is clothed in expensive designer suits and dazzles the congregation with golden rings and private jets. Such concepts distort the reality of Christ within His own Church and are being demolished in our mentality by the forceful advance of the Apostolic Reformation, as the discernment level and quality of the Global Church is taken to a higher level.

The Issues of Apostolic Spheres

In Paul's day, as it is today, false apostles impressed the Church with the boastful announcement of the geographical extent of their apostolic influence, which Paul calls "apostolic measure".

With the multiplication of apostolic networks across the earth as we move further into the 21st century, the removal of limitations to the geographical increase of ministry and the release of global mentality in the Church of Jesus Christ, we are once more in the time when the boastful proclamation of global influence in outwardly seen ministry is becoming the yardstick for the acceptance of apostolic authority and ministry.

Let us examine some principles from Paul concerning an understanding of apostolic spheres.

Wrong Principles Used for Determining Ministry Value
2 Corinthians 10: 12
The company of false apostles used fundamentally wrong principles for determining the value and effectiveness of their ministries in three areas:

▪ *They commended themselves*
They were absorbed in a self-focus that celebrated success according to values they created in their own ministry. The word for "commend" is *'sunistao' (Gk.): to place near to, to set in the same place, to stand near to in order to provide a point of reference.* The word carries the implication of a person providing another with an introduction that gives him acceptability or a point of reference.

It is absolutely important that the apostolic ministry rising in the earth today be scrupulous about acting and speaking only on what is the desire of the Lord for that ministry.

- *They measured themselves by themselves*
No man can create the standard for his own ministry success. We are not the creators or originators of our own work. All that we do comes from the Lord. Any apostolic ministry that does not measure itself according to the standard applied to it by the Kingdom of God and by the Spirit of God is moving in the direction of falsehood.

One of the dangers today of "measuring ourselves by ourselves" is that we can produce ministry that is determined by cultural and environmental factors rather than by the design of the Lord. Let me explain.

In societies such as the United States which has a powerful marketing and communication structure and ability, it is possible for ministry to enter into the *"false strength"* created by marketing, advertising, the easy production and distribution of books, easy availability of finance for overseas travel, access to international television networks and the financial strength of suburban congregations with much personal disposable income. These factors can provide apostles with the natural strength to thrust their ministries far afield and create the false scenario that they are in the perfect will of God. The definition of their measure or apostolic sphere then becomes the product of their personal financial ability to create opportunities, and the ability of their environment to activate them into all kinds of activity.

We must remember that Jesus was not propelled by environmental factors in His ministry in the earth. Sometimes he healed everybody who was sick *(Matthew 8: 16)*. Yet in other cases he selectively healed only a few even though he had the power to heal all who were present and was confronted by a massive human need for healing *(John 5: 2–8)*. His ministry was defined only by the will of the Father at the particular time.

On the other side of the apostolic coin are the valid apostolic ministries in what is called the "3rd world" or lesser developed countries where there is a lack of resources for the promotion of apostolic ministry and building of apostolic spheres.

Here the reality of lack literally shouts to emergent apostolic ministries that they can go no further than their national or regional borders. Many of these apostles have great revelation from the Lord, but it is shut down in the false Babylonian structures of under-development. If they accept what seems to be the limitation of their measure they will never fulfill their mandate from the Lord.

It is necessary for these 3rd world apostles to move their perception to a measure which is declared by the Lord not their environment, and apply supernatural activity in order to "break reality" and escape from their natural limitation into the "spiritual accuracy" of the Lord.

- *They compared themselves among themselves*

This suggests that there was a certain level of competition and rivalry among apostolic camps of the day as they competed for extending of their measures and to exercise dominance over their colleagues.

Such activity will only cause corporate blindness in the various apostolic ministries and networks and there is a real danger of these conditions being repeated today in the Apostolic Reformation as the size and power of apostolic ministries increase. These competitive mentalities open the door for wide-scale satanic distortion of the accuracy of the call of God for our apostolic ministries, and ultimately corrupt and distort the shape of God's global design for the earth. The final impact is to slow down the advance to immortality and to rob the Church of the power to birth divine purpose in the nations of the earth.

Such apostles that do such things "are not wise". The word used here is *'suniemi'(Gk.)* and it suggests not only folly, but a blindness produced by a lack of ability to connect things to each other. It is an inability to relate a cause to an effect; to be completely unaware of the impact produced by incorrect action. In reality it is a destruction of the most essential quality of the apostolic ministry - wisdom.

Paul says, that he refuses to push himself forward in the natural realm and to impress the saints at Corinth with his natural personal force. His warfare will remain in the realm of the spirit – he will not war after the flesh *(2 Corinthians 10: 3)*. Instead he will continue to operate and celebrate the grace of God upon him only within the measure or the apostolic sphere appointed unto him by the Lord.

Apostolic Spheres Have Limits
2 Corinthians 10: 13 - 14

It is important to realize with utmost clarity that apostolic spheres are determined by God Himself. This shaping of these spheres is not constructed from anything that originates from the earth. All natural conditions – ethnicity, nationality, age, size of church, geographical origin are of no impact in the determination of the existence of the spheres of the apostolic.

Our personal testimony is that God has called us from the small Republic of Trinidad and Tobago in the Caribbean and has extended our apostolic sphere through Congress WBN to over 120 nations across the earth.

Each sphere has limits that are determined by God and must not be transgressed by natural power or by force of charisma and personality. There are things that are "beyond measure" or that lie outside of what is the accuracy of God for our global ministry. We may have the ability to perform them but cannot because they are not allowed by the design of God for our ministries. *Rampant expansionism and internationalism of apostolic spheres unrestrained by prophetic discernment is not part of the accuracy of the Lord.*

The word "sphere" *(NKJ; NAU)* or "field" *(NIV)* is the Greek word *'kanon'* defined as follows:

> Kanon : *originally denoted "a straight rod," used as a ruler or measuring instrument ... the secondary notion being either (a) of keeping anything straight ... (b) of testing straightness*

... In general the word thus came to serve for anything regulating the actions of men, as a standard or principle.
Vines Expositionary Dictionary

The suggestion here is that the creation of spheres or *'kanons'* of apostolic authority causes them to become the basic building blocks for the strategic design of God's single purpose for the entire earth *(Isaiah 14:25)*. To violate the orderly arrangement of the spheres by self-willed and ambitious apostolic ministry is to corrupt the general shapes of the divine will for the earth.

Apostles are set in the earth as the "wise master-builders" *(1 Corinthians 3:10)* of the Lord and not only their preaching, teaching and doctrine, but also the very order and shaping of their apostolic measures in the earth contribute to the design of the Lord' s will in the building of Kingdom purpose

Apostolic Spheres are Distributed by God
2 Corinthians 10: 13
The word translated *"appointed"* (NKJ), *"distributed"* (KJV), *"apportioned"* (NAU), *"assigned"* (NIV) is the word *'merizo'*(Gk.): *to divide into parts.* We have already seen that the reality of apostolic spheres points us to a further realization of the strategic activity and design of God's will for all the nations, and the involvement of apostolic ministries as essential 'building' ministries in God's purpose.

This same word is used again by Paul in *1 Corinthians 7:17*:
Only, as the Lord has assigned to each one, as God has called

each, in this manner let him walk. And so I direct in all the churches.

NAU

Nevertheless, each one should retain the place in life that the Lord assigned to him and to which God has called him. This is the rule I lay down in all the churches.

NIV

But as God has distributed to each one, as the Lord has called each one, so let him walk. And so I ordain in all the churches.

NKJ

The various translations of the word *'kanon'* provide us with important insight into the relationship of spheres to the individual apostolic ministries. Each valid apostolic ministry has received a legitimate sphere of activity from the Lord and each ministry should endeavor to "retain" the place that has been provided. Apostles should not shift out of the places assigned to them by God and each should function in the characteristics, special functions, favors and design of ministry facilitated by the apostolic sphere allocated by God.

It is necessary to build and to increase the deposit within the sphere distributed by God.

2 Corinthians 10: 15 - 16

Paul could have proclaimed in the words of today's regional managers of large sales companies: *"Work deeply within the market!"*

Apostolic coverage must not be wide and shallow. It is depth of input that legitimizes movement to a wider sphere. Apostles are not butterflies flitting from flower to flower. The motivating factor of their gifting is the grace to plant and to build. The apostolic initiative seeks to always start a new formulation of the Kingdom of God in any territory which has been entered.

In the Book of Zechariah, the apostolic dimension is represented by Zerubbabel who reduces mountains to level ground and initiates the building by the power of the grace of the Lord:

> 6 *So he answered and said to me: "This is the word of the LORD to Zerubbabel: 'Not by might nor by power, but by My Spirit,' says the LORD of hosts.'*
> 7 *'Who are you, O great mountain? Before Zerubbabel you shall become a plain! And <u>he shall bring forth the capstone with shouts of "Grace, grace to it!'"</u>*
> 8 *Moreover the word of the LORD came to me, saying:*
> 9 *"The hands of Zerubbabel have laid the foundation of this temple; his hands shall also finish it. Then you will know that the LORD of hosts has sent Me to you. ..."*
> **Zechariah 4: 6 – 9 NKJ**

Depth of operation is indicated by the extent to which the "faith is increased" in the hearts of those within the territory who have received the apostolic impartation. An increase of faith means an increase in productivity of Kingdom activity and receptivity to the plans and purposes of the Lord in the area under apostolic invasion. This is not a frivolous activity. Its final intention is that there will be a "finish" to the work. Finishing or the bringing of the work within the territory to full completion is a sign that a sending of the Lord has taken place.

This is a very important concept that contains within it values that are totally contradictory to the Babylonian influences in the church. It is a structure that guarantees Kingdom success. Expansion of apostolic spheres into new areas of spiritual activity is dependent upon full working and faith increase in previous areas of work. Depth of working in a sphere becomes the springboard for advancement into wider fields – apostolic advance becomes a marker for deep Kingdom successes.

The acceptance of such Kingdom values in the midst of the Present Reformation of the Church invalidates apostolic ministry that circles the earth simply to place "more notches in the gun", making visits to nations in which nothing is planted and developed, no faith in the hearts of the saints is increased but reputation is enhanced by quoting how many nations one has visited.

The staging of global conferences simply to make videotapes for distribution and enhancement of reputation is not acceptable to the cause of finishing the purposes of the Lord. The heart of the true apostolic is the extension of the ground of God's workings through the nations by a solid and enduring invasion into the hearts of the people, and the transformation of their mentality permanently by the proclamation of the good news of the Kingdom.

We Cannot Boast Our Way Into Other Men's Labors
2 Corinthians 10:16

Here the word "boast'' means *to take credit* and the issue here is the illegal entering into the accomplishments of another apostolic work by the utilization of the wrong principles. We can associate through relationship and have partnership through agreement, but only to help build the work of the brother with whom we have come into partnership, not to seek credit ourselves in it. Two factors will operate very powerfully in the apostolic networks being developed in the earth today that will remove friction and apostolic collision from the Body of Christ and they are: 1. *Reality of Relationship* and 2. *Recognition of Ranking*.

First let us deal with the issue of the *Reality of Relationship*.

As we advance further into the exciting spiritual realms of the 21st century, as long as global apostolic advance remains on the natural level of linear, geographical definitions, we will continue to have increasing collisions in the earth as apostolic realms and spheres jostle each other.

It is absolutely necessary that global apostolic ministries operate in purity of heart and clarity of motive as the Lord extends their measures over the face of the earth. Kingdom principles must prevail if there is to be no distortion of the Lord's purpose though territorial clashes and global wars for apostolic recognition in various territories of the planet.

We only truly possess that which we do not take ownership over for ourselves. We live only if we die. We only really possess that which we hold lightly with open hands. The principles of the Kingdom are diametrically opposite to the Babylonian principles of the earth. Just as no individual saint can fulfill the requirements of his Kingdom destiny without the participation and involvement of others, and no church can fulfill its corporate destiny without participation from resources outside itself; so too no one apostolic network or apostolic ministry can fulfill its divine mandate without the involvement and partnership of other apostolic resources outside of its borders.

I heard Apostle David Copp Snr. of City at the Cross, Long Beach, California say something at the Congress WBN Global Apostolic Summit in Durban, South Africa in June, 2000, which really registered in my spirit. He said that while Jesus was on the earth in a physical body he was covered with a seamless robe *(John 19: 23 – 24)*. So too must the corporate Body of Christ be robed in a seamless mantle in the earth. This too is a dimension of the mysterious place called the "unity of the faith"*(Ephesians 4:13)* to which we are progressing in the purposes of the Lord.

The clear lines of separation between the activities of diverse authentic apostolic networks must begin to merge into each other, as we migrate to high levels of cooperation and oneness through committed covenants, purity of heart and shared ownership of spiritual resources. The seams in the corporate robe on the Body must begin to disappear as we submerge personal apostolic ministry to the more dynamic and potent corporate apostolic reality of Christ in the Body. Territorial clashes must be non-existent; competition between apostolic spheres must disappear as apostolic leaders in the earth 'buy into' each other's ministries. Apostolic networks in the earth today must become 'laboratories' for the emergence of the spiritual reality of these advanced positions, that will supernaturally move the entire Body toward the grand finalization of the prophetic purposes of Christ in the earth.

Second is the issue of the *Recognition of Ranking*.

Apostles are of varying spiritual rank in the earth. The whole issue of the recognition of rank goes directly to the core of the cancer of self-promotion, pride, inflated ministry egos and self-aggrandizement. The globalization of the Church and the reality of 'apostolic equalization' demand that the spirit of humility be brought to the forefront in operational apostolic ministries in the earth.

The earth will be filled with the knowledge of the glory of the Lord as the waters cover the sea *(Habakkuk 2: 14)*. God has prophetically promised a global dispersion of revelation and knowledge of His ways and purposes. Apostles are being brought forward from all quarters of the earth, both in the developed and under-developed nations, with revelation in their hearts and a word of proclamation in their mouths. Apostolic emergence is being 'equalized' by the Lord.

As the Church increasingly becomes one nation and governmental ministries are given wider spheres by the Lord, it is increasingly necessary for ministries to operate accurately in prophetic discernment of the various rankings and spiritual authority given by the Lord. Only as precise discernment of the ranking of various apostolic ministries is made can we cooperate and give way to apostolic ministries 'invading' our geographical zones. And vice versa, only then can apostolic ministries coming into areas given them by the Lord, relate accurately to apostles that are already placed there and in full operation in the area.

Without purity of heart, reality of covenant relationships and the recognition of varying levels of apostolic ranking, there will be a wilderness of clashing spheres and distortion produced in the spiritual jurisdictions of the earth, by carnal ministries blindly promoting their own works to the detriment of the design and the order of God.

Only He whom the Lord commends is approved
2 Corinthians 10: 18
I have already indicated that the word "commends" indicates the receiving of an introduction or a powerful reference which makes one worthy to be recognized and accepted. No apostolic ministry can commend itself. We all seek the commendation of the Lord, for it is the Lord's commendation that provides us with approval.

The word "approved" is *'dokimos'*. In the days of Paul coins were made by melting precious gold in the furnace and then pouring the molten metal into a mold from which the coin was cast. The rough edges of the coin were then filed and made smooth before the coin entered general circulation. Unscrupulous moneychangers would then file off extra bits of the coin in order to short-change the customer. The coin was still gold and could still be used as currency but its value was diminished unknown to the customer. There were those moneychangers who were honest and would neither receive nor circulate coins that were below the exact stipulated weight. These honest men who became symbols of integrity, true value and straight-fowardness became known as a 'dokimos'. The word 'dokimos' was applied to the coin which was of true weight and also to the moneychanger who handled only coins whose weight was exact and true.

The application to apostolic ministry here is clear and direct. Accurate apostolic ministry seeks to hear from the Lord the testimony that it is regarded as 'dokimos' – exact in principles, proclamation, relationships and doctrine. Such a spiritual rating does not come from man but from the Lord. The eternal principles of the Kingdom of heaven must be applied to apostles and their work in the earth as we move the Church towards the grand climax of the ages.

EIGHT

BUILDING DYNAMIC
APOSTOLIC RELATIONSHIP

The Issue of Effective Following

*L*et us track some instructions given by Paul to his followers telling them some of the fundamental principles for relationship with the apostolic grace:

> ¹⁵ *So then, brothers, <u>stand firm and hold to the teachings</u> we passed on to you, whether by word of mouth or by letter.*
>
> **2 Thessalonians 2:15 NIV**

Apostolic teaching and instruction has to be transmitted and those connected to the apostle are exhorted to "stand firm". The implication is that there will be de-stabilizing forces that will try to cause the followers to slide out of the correctness of the apostolic instruction.

> ¹⁰ *But you have <u>carefully followed</u> my doctrine, manner of life, purpose, faith, longsuffering, love, perseverance,*

---

[14] *But you must continue in the things which you have learned and been assured of, knowing from whom you have learned them*

2 Timothy 3: 10 & 14 NKJ

The instruction to Timothy details the **precise implementation** of apostolic principles and patterns. Paul provides a breakdown of the areas in which Timothy must apply diligent tracking viz:

Doctrine:	Teaching and instruction
Manner of Life:	Lifestyle patterns of the apostle
Purpose:	The divine intent of the apostolic sending
Faith:	Spiritual characteristics and emphases
Longsuffering etc.:	Displayed character

All of these areas indicate that apostolic relationship is not a frivolous activity that is based upon "what can I get for myself" mentalities. Two important things are implied.

First: The apostle must be very conscious that his life, calling, ministry, lifestyle, teaching and conduct provide a dynamic and living pattern to those ordained by God to be in relationship with his apostolic calling. This moves the one called to be an apostle into a place of very conscious conduct of life. He must be very aware of God's requirements for his life and extremely careful to always think and act in such a way that his life provides followers with a conduit to actually "see" the character of God Himself. There is no place here for emphasis on self and self-aggrandizement; no place for deliberate personal elevation and personal ambition; no place for a "my ministry" syndrome.

The single focus of the apostle is the clear and transparent presentation of the truth of God's nature through his life so that those following can have a pattern that demonstrates the nature of Christ as exhibited through the life of the apostle.

Second: Those who follow the apostle must enter into such a relational world that the structures of the apostle's life become very accessible to them. They have to be aware of the teaching, lifestyle and spiritual characteristics of the apostle they are connected to. The Christ patterns in the life of the apostle must be applied to their own lives. They are exhorted to **"carefully follow"**.

The word in Greek used here is *'parakolutheo'* and this word has several shades of meaning:
1. It means "to closely follow and to accompany". This has implications for both discipleship and partnership.
2. It means "to understand" *(to trace the development and the course of a thing)*. This points to a strategic effort to understand the demonstration of Christ in the life of the apostle you are connected to.
3. It means "to conform oneself to a standard followed". This points to entrance into a process of personal development and transformation that aligns itself to the clear biblical standard of Christ that is patterned in the life and conduct of the apostle.

There is great responsibility on both sides of the matter. The apostle as well as the followers have a mandated responsibility to conduct themselves according to the standard of Christ given in the word of God. Paul says:

> Follow my example, as I follow the example of Christ.
>
> **1 Corinthians 11: 1 NIV**

> For you yourselves know how you ought to follow our example...
>
> **2 Thessalonians 3: 7 NIV**

It is very clear that the starting responsibility is the integrity that must be found in the apostle's life. The patterns of Christ must be so clearly followed in his life that those who follow him will find themselves walking in the exact biblical patterns of Christ-likeness.

Five (5) Essential Principles for Apostolic Relationship

Let us look into the Word of God to discover several clear principles that indicate how apostolic relationship is built.

1. *We Must Access Apostolic Doctrine*
Acts 2: 42 - 43 NKJ
   [42] *And they continued steadfastly in the apostles' doctrine and fellowship, in the breaking of bread, and in prayers.*
   [43] *Then fear came upon every soul (new spiritual culture), and many wonders and signs were done (expressions of God) through the apostles.*

Diligence in following is required in those who connect to an apostolic grace. They must "continue steadfastly". The original word used here indicates high levels of attentiveness and focus.

There must be great clarity about the emphases of the apostle in teaching the word of God. Each apostolic person has a different emphasis and focus as God designs the purpose for which they have been called. This produces a particular emphasis in the Word of God which followers must be aware of and pay attention to.

Fellowship and community is important. Spiritual activity like prayer by all those connected is also important to build a consistent spiritual culture and to join people into one single mission before God. As this was done in the early days of the Acts of the Apostles in Jerusalem the fear of God fell on the people. There was a definite community awareness that God was with them and God began to express Himself through the works of the apostles among the people.

In the light of this we can suggest some important personal considerations that every Senior Pastor should engage in:
- I must discover and determine who is the apostolic resource that I am ordained to connect with:
- I must develop strategies to access the apostolic resources.
- I must operate by clearly defined biblical principles in doing this.

2. We Must Follow Apostolic Ways
1 Corinthians 4: 16 - 17 NKJ
16 *Therefore I urge you, imitate me.*
17 *For this reason I have sent Timothy to you, who is my beloved and faithful son in the Lord, who will remind you of* <u>*my ways in Christ*</u>*, as I teach everywhere in every church.*

Timothy was very familiar with Paul's "ways in Christ" and was able to remind the church at Corinth about those particular apostolic ways. The word used is *'hodos'* (Gk): *pathways in the Spirit; systems of spiritual culture; methods for doing things; unique characteristics and standards for operations.*

This is important apostolic technology. Each apostle called and commissioned by the Lord has a defined "way" *(hodos)* in Christ. Each has a particular and unique anointing, system of operation, defined spiritual emphasis that has been designed and given by the Lord Himself. There is a clear way in which things are done. Closely related followers, such as Timothy was to Paul, are able to define the "ways" to others who have come into connection and can actually teach them in a systematic way so that others can understand not just the individual called to be an apostle but more important the apostolic system and design that has been given by the Lord through the individual apostle's life to the people. Paul himself taught his ways in Christ "everywhere in every church".

Followers were urged to "imitate". This is not mindless following of a man but it refers to the identification and association with clear Christ principles in an apostle who God has ordained to be in relationship with you. Following those Christ principles is godly, approved imitation. This is such an important and vital condition. Leaders and saints are only exhorted to diligently follow an apostle only as long as the apostle clearly and manifestly follows Christ himself in a way that all the followers can observe and pattern themselves after. In this way we follow the Lord and not just a human person.

Such accurate following produces honorable representation of the apostolic and distribution of apostolic standards and life in all of the churches. It is clear from the scripture that there was a definite and deliberate effort by Paul and his closest disciples to cause widespread distribution of the apostolic standards throughout all the churches connected to Paul's apostolic grace. So that in the end the apostolic dimension is not in the characteristic of an individual man but becomes an operational principle in the churches by accurate and faithful representation.

*Whatever you have **learned** or **received** or **heard** from me, or **seen** in me-- put it into practice. And the God of peace will be with you.*

Philippians 4: 9 NIV

The Word of God does not leave us guessing but provides clear patterns that we can follow into accurate and productive following of apostolic patterns. We are given instructions and we are told to put them into practice. Here we are given four different levels of accessing.

Four Different Levels of Accessing
- Learned or Instruction
- Received or Impartation
- Heard / Report or Information
- Seen or Manifestation

A Senior Leader of a Kingdom Community with the Leadership Team can now engage in strategic development of activity in each of these areas provided above for there to be systematic downloading of apostolic grace. This is an area for interesting and vigorous discussion by leadership teams of churches as they develop the nature of their association and connection to an apostolic grace. These defined areas have to be "put into practice" and the net result is that the "God of peace will be with you".

3. There Must be Depth of Apostolic Relationship

Here a crisis emerges for the church at Ephesus. Paul is on his way to Jerusalem and great personal crisis awaits him in the city. He has arrived at the end of his ministry on earth and will soon be killed in Rome. On his journey to Jerusalem he arrives at the port city of Miletus on the ship and sends for the elders of the church at Ephesus. They gather to him in Miletus and Paul announces to them the end of his apostolic relationship with the church and informs them of the serious spiritual dangers that will come upon the community after he departs from them.

17 *From Miletus, Paul sent to Ephesus for the elders of the church.*

18 *When they arrived, he said to them: "You know how I lived the whole time I was with you, from the first day I came into the province of Asia.*

19 *I served the Lord with great humility and with tears and in the midst of severe testing by the plots of my Jewish opponents.*

20 *You know that I have not hesitated to preach anything that would be helpful to you but have taught you publicly and from house to house.*

22 *"And now, compelled by the Spirit, I am going to Jerusalem, not knowing what will happen to me there.*

²³ *I only know that in every city the Holy Spirit warns me that prison and hardships are facing me.*

²⁵ *"Now I know that none of you among whom I have gone about preaching the kingdom will ever see me again.*

²⁶ *Therefore, I declare to you today that I am innocent of the blood of any of you.*

²⁷ *For I have not hesitated to proclaim to you the whole will of God. ..."*

Acts 20: 17 – 20, 22 – 23, 25 – 27 NIV

This is a catastrophic event for the community at Ephesus because the removal of Paul's apostolic covering of the church will transform their spiritual environment and cause unstable conditions to occur:

²⁹ *I know that after I leave, savage wolves will come in among you and will not spare the flock.*

³⁰ *Even from your own number men will arise and distort the truth in order to draw away disciples after them.*

³¹ *So be on your guard!*

Acts 20: 29 – 31   NIV

But even in the face of such horrible news, the dangers from the dark realm of the spirit is not their primary concern. They are being cut off from their cherished apostolic relationship. They love Paul and they follow him down to the ship as he departs from them. They are weeping in sorrow:

³⁶ *When Paul had finished speaking, he knelt down with all of them and prayed.*

³⁷ *They all wept as they embraced him and kissed him.*

38 What grieved them most was his statement that they would never see his face again. Then they accompanied him to the ship.

Acts 20: 36 – 38 NIV

This is a beautiful biblical pattern for the relationship between an apostolic resource and the churches put under his care by God. This is a perfected Kingdom relationship in all its loveliness! Truth, honesty, clarity and integrity lie at the heart of this amazing scene at the docks of Miletus. More than anything else this scene demonstrates the God-approved purity of a correct apostolic relationship.

4. We Must Share in the Apostolic Grace
Philippians 1: 3 – 7 NIV
3 I thank my God every time I remember you.
4 In all my prayers for all of you, I always pray with joy
5 because of your partnership in the gospel from the first day until
6 being confident of this, that he who began a good work in you will carry it on to completion until the day of Christ Jesus.
7 It is right for me to feel this way about all of you, since (a) I have you in my heart (b) all of you share in God's grace with me.

Ephesians 3: 2 NKJ
*… if indeed you have heard of the dispensation of the grace of God which was **given to me for you**,…*

The scriptures are very clear. The grace that comes from the Lord and is delivered into the life of an apostle has to be shared with the saints. The apostle is simply the conduit or the channel for the divine resource. The intent of God is clearly to place an apostolic impartation upon the church. God is more concerned with the **Dimension of the Apostolic** released to the saints than about the individual apostle himself.

The **Apostolic Dimension** is the widespread distribution of apostolic grace to the general Body of Christ in order to strengthen and stabilize it. It causes significant apostolic characteristics such as spiritual maturity, knowledge and ability to function generally in the life of each Kingdom believer. So we can say that the purpose of the apostle is **to impart to the church the grace that is upon him** to produce spiritual maturity in the saints. That which is given can and should be shared.

*I long to see you so that I may impart to you some spiritual gift to make you strong (so that you may be **established**. NKJ)*

Romans 1: 11 NIV

The word "impart" is *'metadidomi'* (Gk): to give a share of. It is Paul's deep desire to travel to the church in Rome to give them a share of what has come down from heaven upon his life. This is the accuracy of the apostolic desire! At its core it is communal and not selfish. Coded into the apostolic grace that fell from heaven is the spirit and attitude of otherness and the willingness to distribute to all what one has received from the Lord above. Thus to impart is to allow others to partake together with you of what is originally yours.

The result of this powerful impartation would be the "establishment" of the church in Rome. The church would be "set in place with strength, or fixed firmly in place". The outflow of the grace of the apostle would bring great benefit to the church and we can clearly see how the release of the apostolic grace is a significant feature of the building activity of the Lord within the Body of Christ.

These truths help us to calibrate our understanding of what is the heart and working of the true apostolic in the earth today, but they also assist us in discerning what is frivolous, selfish and false, posturing itself as an apostolic functionality but not adhering to the clear principles declared in the word of God. Clearly declared truth in the Word of God enables the discernment capability of the saints.

The shared grace of the apostolic sets a standard for building of God's purposes within the Body of Christ. The teaching of Paul; is that the apostolic grace is foundational:

> ¹⁰ *By the grace God has given me, I laid a foundation as a wise builder, and <u>someone else is building on it</u>. But each one should build with care.*
> ¹¹ *For no one can lay any foundation other than the one already laid, which is Jesus Christ.*
> ¹² *If anyone builds on this foundation using gold, silver, costly stones, wood, hay or straw,*
> ¹³ *their work will be shown for what it is, because the Day will bring it to light. It will be revealed with fire, and the fire will test the quality of each person's work.*
> **1 Corinthians 3: 10 – 13 NIV**

The building grace of the apostolic is given to the apostle by the Lord. This grace is not self-generated. It either comes from the Lord or else it is an illusion. It enables the apostle to use his life and his teaching to form a foundation in the churches upon which everything else can be securely built. The foundation IS Jesus Christ. The lifestyle and teaching is Word-based and clearly demonstrating and proclaiming Christ not the opinion and pet dream-spasms of the apostle.

Upon this foundation of Christ others connected to the apostle can build with faith and confidence. They must "build with care" respecting and honoring the value of the foundation laid. There is a quality demand and a responsibility factor. Whatever is built will be evaluated and tested by the Lord on the final Day. The sharing of the apostolic grace imposes a deep and profound responsibility upon those who receive it. They must build with quality and strive to honor the Lord completely with their receiving of the grace and the output from their lives as a result of the receiving.

5. *We Must Enter into Financial Relationship*
    Philippians 4: 17 - 19 NIV
    17 Not that I am looking for a gift, but I am looking for what may be credited to your account.
    18 I have received full payment and even more; I am amply supplied, now that I have received from Epaphroditus the gifts you sent. They are a fragrant offering (a sweet-smelling aroma), an acceptable sacrifice, pleasing to God.
    19 And my God will meet all your needs according to his glorious riches in Christ Jesus.

Giving represented the care for the apostle and for the apostolic mission. The gift causes a definite biblical spiritual release – blessing would multiply towards them. This would be more than simply a monetary activity. The finance was described as a sweet smelling aroma; a fragrant offering; an acceptable sacrifice that was pleasing to God.

This giving of finance would be consequent upon the fact that all the other conditions of relationship with the apostolic were in place. Then the giving of finance became an act of priesthood, sanctified and honoring to the Lord. Here the monetary gift translates into spiritual power; the pleasure of God is manifested in the hearts of the givers and heavenly power is released to supply the needs of those who are correctly connected.

This is often misquoted scripture! Paul says in the letter to the Philippians that because of the correct giving of the correctly connected Philippian church that "**my God**" will supply "<u>your needs</u>". The monetary gift plugged the church into the supply and apostolic resource system of Paul himself before God. They would access the power of the God of Paul and their local and immediate needs would be met by a resource that operated on a higher spiritual level than they themselves. They would tap completely into a powerful apostolic supply. The spiritual technology declared here by Paul is staggering in its beauty and complexity. It makes the transactional reality of giving and receiving honorable and fulfilling. It is the perfect closure to a full understanding of the amazing nature of the apostolic grace!

NINE

UNDERSTANDING APOSTOLIC NETWORKS

A Leadership Principle

*F*undamental to the reality of a correctly functioning apostolic network is the fact that there must be a called and spiritually functional Primary Apostle placed in the context of a surrounding Apostolic Team. The functioning of a team is a Core Leadership Principle in the Kingdom of God. God is a team – Father, Son and Holy Spirit. Each member of the Godhead has a distinct personality and functionality but are all equally God, none is superior to the other. However it is clear that the Father is the head of the Team and a correct order of ranking prevails:

> 24 *Then the end will come, when he (Jesus) hands over the kingdom to God the Father after he has destroyed all dominion, authority and power.*

²⁵ For he must reign until he has put all his enemies under his feet.

²⁶ The last enemy to be destroyed is death.

²⁷ For he "has put everything under his feet." Now when it says that "everything" has been put under him, it is clear that this does not include God himself, who put everything under Christ.

²⁸ When he has done this, then the Son himself will be made subject to him who put everything under him, so that God may be all in all.

1 Corinthians 15: 24 – 28 NIV

Jesus will submit everything unto the power and authority of the Father so that God may be all in all! **It is clear that headship is not superiority** for though Father is the ranking head of the God-team He is not more God than the Holy Spirit nor is the Holy Spirit less divine than Jesus, although he speaks not of himself but testifies of what Christ has said already to us. Jesus said:

"But when the Helper comes, whom I shall send to you from the Father, the Spirit of truth who proceeds from the Father, He will testify of Me. ..."

John 15: 26 NKJ

So the Kingdom of God presents us with profound principles that are completely oppositional to the principles of the Babylonian world system. In the Babylon world system there is hierarchy in which the one who is above is superior and exercises power over those below him. However, the Kingdom does not work by a system of hierarchy but by systems of spiritual ranking, in which one may be functionally in a place of greater authority, but yet all are equal in standing and status before God. Though our Savior Jesus is the Son of God yet we have been all made sons unto God through the power of salvation – *"For you are all sons of God through faith in Christ Jesus."* *(Galatians 3:26)*

Ranking thus allows strong leadership but at the same time upholds the core principle of brotherhood and equality before God. This has to be spiritually discerned and cannot be understood if looked at through the carnal lens of the Babylon world system. When the correct system of ranking is implemented in an apostolic network it permits leadership with humility; oversight with a spirit of serving; government from a place of brotherhood, mutual respect and honoring; direction from a place of death to self.

25 *Jesus called them together and said, "You know that the rulers of the Gentiles lord it over them, and their high officials exercise authority over them.*

26 *Not so with you. Instead, whoever wants to become great among you must be your servant,*

27 *and whoever wants to be first must be your slave--*

28 *just as the Son of Man did not come to be served, but to serve, and to give his life as a ransom for many."*

Matthew 20: 25 – 28 NIV

Network Definitions

An Apostolic Network is a gathering of self-governing Kingdom Communities that are voluntarily united around a common vision determined by a called, gifted and spiritually functioning apostle. **However, it is important to recognize that being part of an Apostolic Network in no way compromises the integrity of the unique vision of each individual community.** In fact, in the correct forms of networking it is required that each community must come forward with its own particular and unique vision, culture and definition in the Lord.

An Apostolic Network is a platform that encourages individuality, the pursuit of personal vision and the unique vision of the local communities, creativity and the freedom to listen to God and do as He demands. This is something that is frequently misunderstood. At the same time, it affords the privilege of being joined to a wider vision with core operational platforms of Apostolic Grace and Apostolic Relationship.

No apostle has the authority to hijack the vision and the purpose of a local assembly that is connected to him. The apostle does not have the authority to usurp the power of the local pastor and to take control of the operations of a local church without proper cause.

Apostolic authority is only exercised when it is voluntarily received and promoted within the local community by the leadership of that community. That authority cannot be imposed. Once the local leadership rejects the authority of the apostle all rights to exercise directive authority in that local community immediately cease.

The relationships in an Apostolic Network are not synthetic, legislated or event-oriented but committed, covenantal and purpose driven. The connection between the apostle and the leaders and saints of a local community come from the heart:

> *6 ...being confident of this very thing, that He who has begun a good work in you will complete it until the day of Jesus Christ;*
>
> *7 just as it is right for me to think this of you all, because I have you in my heart, inasmuch as both in my chains and in the defense and confirmation of the gospel, you all are partakers with me of grace.*

> **Philippians 1: 6 – 7 NKJ**

Network relationships are "uncovered or discovered not made or created". It must be the will of God that one is ordained by God to be connected in a life-giving connection to a particular apostolic resource. When a person comes into connection with an apostolic resource, that person is entering an arrangement that has been pre-ordained by the Lord. In that sense you do not determine of yourself to join an Apostolic Network. It is in this context that we say that connection is "discovered" and "found" by the person desiring to be connected. The network is in fact the reality of joined lives all ordained by God to be connected in relationship with a particular apostolic resource.

Entry into the network is through the recognition and relationship with the apostolic grace in whatever dimension of plurality that expresses itself in. Because of that joining there is thus a consequent covenant brotherhood of all those joined to the same apostolic grace.

Benefits of Apostolic Networking

Personal Development
Proverbs 13: 20 NKJ
He who walks with wise men will be wise, but the companion of fools will be destroyed.

This is impartation by association. The apostolic is associated with wisdom. Paul described the grace that came upon him from the Lord as making him a "wise master builder" *(1 Corinthians 3: 10)*. Here wisdom is skill, competence, knowledge and clarity in the things of the Lord for advancing the purposes of the Kingdom. Association with the wisdom of the apostolic causes upgrade and a definite increase in competence of the one connecting.

Strength in Warfare
Ezekiel 32: 2 – 4 NIV
[2] *"Son of man, take up a lament concerning Pharaoh king of Egypt and say to him: "'You are like a lion among the nations; you are like a monster in the seas thrashing about in your streams, churning the water with your feet and muddying the streams.*
[3] *"'This is what the Sovereign LORD says: "'With a great throng of people I will cast my net over you, and they will haul you up in my net.*
[4] *I will throw you on the land and hurl you on the open field. I will let all the birds of the sky settle on you and all the animals of the wild gorge themselves on you. ...'"*

In this scripture networking a throng of people causes massive increase of strength and power to prevail over a terrible enemy. Though Pharaoh is like a lion in the nations and a monster in the seas he is no match for the connected strength of the net of God.

Leviticus 26: 7 - 8 NIV
7 You will pursue your enemies, and they will fall by the sword before you.
8 Five of you will chase a hundred, and a hundred of you will chase ten thousand, and your enemies will fall by the sword before you.

Here strength exponentially increases as people network together. It seems that heavenly prevailing power is added to the human factor as the numbers increase. This is a community battle not an individual conflict. We can do and achieve much more together than is possible if we remain alone.

Stronger Prayer Power Operations
Matthew 18: 19 - 20 NIV
19 "Again, truly I tell you that if two of you on earth agree about anything they ask for, it will be done for them by my Father in heaven.
20 For where two or three gather in my name, there am I with them."

Coming together causes an intensity of the Presence of God in the midst far beyond what is possible if one stands before God alone. Once more is revealed the mysterious power of community. Agreement requires there to be more than one, but it also requires that people get together on the same spiritual frequency. Agreement is a feature of effective apostolic networking and it causes connection to be made mightily between the request coming up from the earth and the divine resources and response descending from heaven. Once more we can see the internal explosive power of correct and effective apostolic networking.

An Increase in Accountability, Productivity, Accuracy
Ecclesiastes 4: 9 – 12 NIV

9 Two are better than one, because they have a good return for their labor:

10 If either of them falls down, one can help the other up. But pity anyone who falls and has no one to help them up.

11 Also, if two lie down together, they will keep warm. But how can one keep warm alone?

12 Though one may be overpowered, two can defend themselves. A cord of three strands is not quickly broken.

The benefits of networking or coming together here are immense. The productivity of work in spiritual things increases as we work together. There is mutual encouragement, support and strengthening provided when we stand together. And once more we see that there is great strength in battle and the more the network increases the more spiritually intimidating it becomes to the enemy for "a cord of three strands is not quickly broken."

Access to Divine Attention and Favor
Malachi 3: 16 – 17 NIV

16 *Then those who feared the LORD talked with each other, and the LORD listened and heard. A scroll of remembrance was written in his presence concerning those who feared the LORD and honored his name.*

17 *"On the day when I act," says the LORD Almighty, "they will be my treasured possession. I will spare them, just as a father has compassion and spares his son who serves him. ..."*

It is the connectivity that creates the divine attention. The people have something in common – they feared the Lord and honored His name and thus communicated with each other out of that common bond. This is the power of the network! The mutuality and the connection in the earth cause powerful movements in the heavenly realms - God takes a record of them.

This relates directly to the practice of the ancient eastern kings who would write up the exploits of a person in a book of remembrance. Many years later when another king sat on the throne he would call for the book of remembrance and would see the name of the person inscribed who performed great things long before he came to the throne. In that day he would honor the descendants of that person and shower them with favor, gifts and treasure. The spiritual connectivity of correct apostolic networking causes divine favor to fall heavily upon us.

Activation of Last Day Realities
Zechariah 8: 20 – 21 & 23 NKJ

20 *This is what the LORD Almighty says ...*

21 *"... the inhabitants of one city will go to another and say, 'Let us go at once to entreat the LORD and seek the LORD Almighty. I myself am going.'..."*

....

23 *" In those days ten people from all languages and nations will take firm hold of one Jew by the hem of his robe and say, 'Let us go with you, because we have heard that God is with you.'"*

These scriptures take us into the times of the end and we can see that networking is an integral feature of the architecture of the times. The inhabitants of one city will go to another – connection is made. Seeking and entreating the Lord is a community activity not an isolated act. The life of the Kingdom over and over in the Word of God is presented as the powerful connection of people of like mind coming together before the Lord. The strength of the movement of the Kingdom in the times of the End is enshrined in the hearts of saints of like mind coming together in agreement before the Lord.

Principles from David

David and the principles enshrined in his life are powerful icons of the Kingdom of God. Jesus as King and Ruler is closely associated in scripture with the throne of David:

31 *"...And behold, you will conceive in your womb and bring forth a Son, and shall call His name JESUS.*

32 *He will be great, and will be called the Son of the Highest; and the Lord God will give Him the throne of His father David.*

³³ *And He will reign over the house of Jacob forever, and of His kingdom there will be no end."*

Luke 1: 31 – 33 NKJ

David's movement to become the king of Judah is very closely associated with networking principles as mighty warriors gathered around him. Thus we can say that networking is at the very core of the formation of the principles of the Kingdom.

¹ Now these were the men who came to David at Ziklag while he was still a fugitive from Saul the son of Kish; and they were among the mighty men, helpers in the war, ...

....

³⁸ All these men of war, who could keep ranks, came to Hebron with a loyal heart, to make David king over all Israel; and all the rest of Israel were of one mind to make David king.

1 Chronicles 12: 1 & 38 NKJ

In looking into the mobilization of mighty men around David as a powerful network was built that would elevate him to the throne, we can identify several important principles that we can apply to the reality of apostolic networks.

Core of Network is the Discernment of a Spiritual Position and Resource

*"These were the men who came to David at Ziklag **while he was still a fugitive from Saul**"* These mighty warriors were not drawn to David because of his wealth, fame, popularity or esteem. He was still a fugitive living in a cave in Ziklag but these mighty men discerned the call of the Lord and the appointment of the Lord upon David. They came not for what they could get but

for what they could offer to the divine purpose. This is a pristine and necessary reality for effective apostolic networking.

There was Great Purity of Motive
1 Chronicles 12: 16 - 17 NKJ

16 Then some of the sons of Benjamin and Judah came to David at the stronghold.

17 And David went out to meet them, and answered and said to them, "If you have come peaceably to me to help me, my heart will be united with you; but if to betray me to my enemies, since there is no wrong in my hands, may the God of our fathers look and bring judgment."

There was a condition given by David for the uniting of their hearts. They had to have come in peace and with purity of motive. David declares that there is no wrong in his hands. The environment of connection was filled with purity and sanctity. The environment could not be polluted. David calls on God to look upon their coming together and to judge any uncleanness.

There was a Commitment to Acts of Courage and Valor
1 Chronicles 12: 14 - 15 NKJ

14 These were from the sons of Gad, captains of the army; the least was over a hundred, and the greatest was over a thousand.

15 These are the ones who crossed the Jordan in the first month, when it had overflowed all its banks; and they put to flight all those in the valleys, to the east and to the west.

These men were all powerful warriors. There was not one weak among them. The least of them was over a hundred men – all had capacity; all were filled with courage and all were willing to fight in the most adverse conditions. This was a gathering of strength not a celebration of weakness. There are massive principles for apostolic networking here!

Connections Were Inspired by the Holy Spirit
1 Chronicles 12: 18 NKJ
18 Then the Spirit came upon Amasai, chief of the captains, and he said: "We are yours, O David; We are on your side, O son of Jesse! Peace, peace to you, And peace to your helpers! For your God helps you." So David received them, and made them captains of the troop.

One version of this verse says that the Spirit "clothed himself with Amasai". Nothing is natural about this connection that is being made. It is elevated to the level of spirit-birthed covenant. The human connection between David and Amasai is accurate in the mind and will of God and so the Spirit of God participates deeply in the formation of this new networking relationship.

David's Network on Earth Manifested the Presence of God
1 Chronicles 12: 22 NKJ
For at that time they came to David day by day to help him, until it was a great army, like the army of God.
There is progressive development of the gathering around David and things grow over time. Addition to the group of warriors was determined by the purity of heart and motive. It was superintended by the presence of the Holy Spirit and activated by the calling and commissioning that was upon the life of David. As the Davidic Network grew progressively so did the presence and the power of God manifesting on the earth

until it seemed that God was encamped in the midst of them. Though David gathered them, the true king in the midst of them was God Himself and the view from the heavens was that this was in fact the army of God encamped about him in the earth.

This is perhaps the most precious image of a mature and correctly functioning Apostolic Network. The gathering of covenant must come to a state of maturity in which the earthly leaders and the anointings given to them by God are not as prominent as the Divine values, character, mission and presence that fills the network. The network must, as David's did, become the encampment of God and it must shine forth with biblical principles flowing from the lives of all. Thus is God honored and glorified in an apostolic environment.

TEN

APOSTOLIC PRINCIPLES

FOR THE HARVEST

I
Defining Harvest

The Harvest is the End of the Age - Matthew 13: 39

*P*owerful words are used here. The word "end" is *'sunteleia'* (Gk): denoting the events leading up to a climax. The word "age" is *'aion'* (Gk) pointing to a definite period of time which demands that certain events take place. When put together we are speaking of a time when specific and definite events begin to occur which inevitably lead to a climax. Therefore, the harvest is not just an event but also a process that leads to the eventual event. It is not just an evangelistic event but also the sum total of all the activity that will propel the ages to an ultimate climax.

Principles of the Process

Harvest cannot be separated from a definite process and is bound up with the idea of a Finish. In the Old Testament harvest was the culmination of the agricultural cycle – a set of different processes that ended in the joy of reaping. So, harvest is the sum collection of mentalities, understandings, positions, revelations, insights and activities, that will propel the ages towards the ultimate climax. This is the Harvest!

We can look into the speaking of Jesus about the harvest and extract several relevant principles. Jesus is teaching in the villages and towns of Judea and he looks upon the suffering of the people as he heals their diseases and infirmities:

> ³⁶ *When he saw the crowds, he had compassion on them, because they were harassed and helpless, like sheep without a shepherd.*
> ³⁷ *Then he said to his disciples, "The harvest is plentiful but the workers are few.*
> ³⁸ *Ask the Lord of the harvest, therefore, to send out workers into his harvest field."*
> ### *Matthew 9: 36 – 38 NIV*

Issues of perspective are important here. Jesus is gazing upon the crowds or the multitudes. This is significant of vast vision or of extensive Kingdom concern. He sees the state of the people – harassed; helpless and without a shepherd. The words used in the original language carry extended meanings:

- **_Harassed_** (Weary NKJ): *'skullo'* – to skin, to tear into, to vex, to trouble and annoy

- *__Helpless__* (Scattered NKJ): *'rhipto'* – to throw down to the ground, to cast down without care, to set down hastily
- *__No shepherd__*: leadership issues – the multitudes are destroyed because there is no vision or direction propelling them forward.

This is what Jesus perceives and this is what He responds to and we must keep in mind that when we track the mentality, vision, actions and responses of Jesus Christ we are tracking what should be the mentality, vision, actions and responses of ourselves. We must be like Him!

The response of Jesus is to send out (*'ekballo'*) workers into the harvest. The word means – to drive out with force and power; to propel violently; to cast out with strength. The harvest overpowers the workers – *verse 37*. They are few: (*in number but also slight in size and weak in intensity*). The harvest demands a new kind of worker who is cast out into (among, towards) the harvest. They are not only sent with force but they also manifest the character of their unique sending in the harvest itself.

Jesus commands the release of the harvest technology of prayer to activate a forceful divine initiative from the Lord of the Harvest to send out forceful laborers into the harvest. Prayer is the force that destroys the imbalance between the magnitude of the work and the resources to accomplish it.

The Apostolic Solution

The personal response of Jesus Himself is of critical importance and has relevance to our understanding of apostolic things in the Body of Christ today. *Matthew 9: 36 – 38* identifies the massive problem that is viewed by Jesus. But in Chapter 10 he moves to provide the definite solution to the problem.

Matthew Chapter 10 is the "sending out" chapter. Here for the first time Jesus moves his disciples into an apostolic position. Here he equips them, activates them and sends them out into the harvest work of the Kingdom. Never again after this are they called disciples. They are now moved to another spiritual position and they begin to advance the work of the Kingdom. So the response of Jesus Himself is to release apostolic anointings through an apostolic people, into the harvest, for apostolic breakthrough results.

The required Last Day Harvest Apostolic Mentality is clear:
- There must be a clear discerning of global conditions.
- There must be the conviction that we have the solution and that we are the answer to the groans of the world.
- There must be the authority of a prayer release that causes a divine decision to release apostolic initiatives propelled with force into the harvest.

Jesus continues to speak of mentalities that are necessary in the days of Harvest – the end of the age:
> 34 *Jesus said to them, "My food is to do the will of Him who sent Me, and to finish His work.*
> 35 *Do you not say, 'There are still four months and then comes the harvest'? Behold, I say to you, lift up your eyes (wake up (NLT)) and look at the fields, for they are already white for harvest! ..."*
>
> **John 4: 34 – 35 NKJ**

To "do the will" and "finish the work" – both activities are inextricably linked. Any doing must be done with the desire to finish. To finish is: *to add what is missing in order to render a thing complete or full / to carry through to the absolute end / to bring to a close by event.*

This statement by Jesus releases to us what can be called the **Apostolic Paradigm** for the days in which we live. He tells us that:

- **The embedded reality of the earth can be broken**. It is authorized by God – *"But I say to you" (verse 35)*. The systems of the earth and time proclaim one thing – that a movement to the Finish, the arrival at Harvest is impossible; but the speaking from Heaven says something entirely different. It is a matter of the superiority of spiritual vision. This clash of perspectives involves the collision of two different realities. Both realities exist in the earth now!

- **The Word of God has to be given a higher reality than your proven experience** – this is the realm of faith – *the substance of things hoped for; the evidence of things not yet seen (Hebrews 11: 1)*

- ***"Lift up your eyes and Look!"*** *(verse 35)* Conscious deliberate activity is needed. You **HAVE** to *"wake up"* / *"lift up your eyes"*. We have to elevate our sight-lines in an apostolic day and *"look around"* – deliberately regard the structure of the spirit-realm. We have to see, as accomplished, the purpose and intent of God – and it will be so!

In *John 4: 36 – 37* Jesus makes a startling pronouncement concerning the harvest:

> 36 *Even now the one who reaps draws a wage and harvests a crop for eternal life, so that the sower and the reaper may be glad together.*
> 37 *Thus the saying 'One sows and another reaps' is true.*
>
> **John 4: 36 – 37 NIV**

The Harvest is the end of the cycle of producing Kingdom fruit and both the sower and the reaper must be glad together. The beginning *(the sower)* and the ending *(the reaper)* are connected in the context of the harvest. The beginning and the end must be of the same principle, strength, character, quality and faith as the nature of the beginning of the thing started since Genesis. We must enter into the harvest with ancient mentalities and with the fire and intensity of the prophets and patriarchs of old.

There has to pour forth from the global church a new spirit, not a modern spirit but the attitude and faith that drove men of old to do extreme exploits for God and to impact nations by the power of the word. This is facilitated by God with the massive release of apostolic grace to the Body of Christ today.

II
Harvest Meanings in the Word of God

A Time of Gathering and Bringing Things Together
Proverbs 6: 6 – 8 NIV
6 Go to the ant, you sluggard; consider its ways and be wise!
7 It has no commander, no overseer or ruler,
8 yet it stores its provisions in summer and gathers its food at harvest.

A Time of Watchfulness and Spiritual Vigilance
Proverbs 10: 5 NIV
He who gathers crops in summer is a prudent son, but he who sleeps during harvest is a disgraceful son.

A Time of Reward for the Diligent Worker
Proverbs 20: 4 NLT
Those too lazy to plow in the right season will have no food at the harvest.

A Time of Joy, Deliverance and Broken Yokes
Isaiah 9: 2- 4 NLT
2 The people who walk in darkness will see a great light. For those who live in a land of deep darkness, a light will shine.
3 You will enlarge the nation of Israel, and its people will rejoice. They will rejoice before You as people rejoice at the harvest and like warriors dividing the plunder.
4 For You will break the yoke of their slavery and lift the heavy burden from their shoulders.

A Time of Caring, Remembrance, Humility and Mercy

In *Deuteronomy 24: 19 – 22* the harvest was to be reaped with a spirit of compassion and humility. The people were commanded to remember the days of their own servitude and dispossession. It was filled with a spirit of humility in the awareness that redemption was not achieved through their own strength but was the fruit of God's mercy to them:

> 19 *"When you are harvesting your crops and forget to bring in a bundle of grain from your field, don't go back to get it. Leave it for the foreigners, orphans, and widows. Then the LORD your God will bless you in all you do.*
>
> 20 *When you beat the olives from your olive trees, don't go over the boughs twice. Leave the remaining olives for the foreigners, orphans, and widows.*
>
> 21 *When you gather the grapes in your vineyard, don't glean the vines after they are picked. Leave the remaining grapes for the foreigners, orphans, and widows.*
>
> 22 *Remember that you were slaves in the land of Egypt. That is why I am giving you this command.*
>
> **Deuteronomy 24: 19 – 22 NLT**

A Time of Crossing and Fulfillment of Covenant Promises

Joshua led the people through Jordan's overflowing banks in the time of harvest. God brought them from the dry wilderness into a time of plenty. It was a day of new leadership replacing the old. They crossed into a day of manifestation and covenant realization of the promises of God.

---

14 So it was, when the people set out from their camp to cross over the Jordan, with the priests bearing the ark of the covenant before the people,
15 and as those who bore the ark came to the Jordan, and the feet of the priests who bore the ark dipped in the edge of the water (for the Jordan overflows all its banks during the whole time of harvest), ...

Joshua 3: 14 15 NKJ

A Time of Honorable Manhood, Exact Protocol and Divine Order

In the Book of Ruth there is an awesome presentation of the harvest. Here those that are empty are filled and bitter lives are made sweet. Boaz (a picture of Christ) at last finds the perfect bride (Church). It is the season of the Kingdom society functioning without conflict and according to biblical law as Boaz and the close relative exchange sandals to bring the redemption of Ruth to absolute perfection. It is a day of generosity, hope and corporate rejoicing.

All of these are principles and pictures of the Apostolic Age of Harvest into which we are now entering. It is a day of joy and spiritual maturity; a season of clear and accurate leadership; it is a time when the saints with a sense of participation and responsibility rise to move the things of the Kingdom forward with great momentum in the will of God!

When the princes in Israel take the lead, when the people willingly offer themselves-- praise the LORD!

Judges 5:2 NIV

APPENDIX

SOME DEFINERS
OF THE APOSTOLIC
REFORMATION

*T*he current Move of God in the Body of Christ across the earth today is called The Apostolic Reformation. It is Apostolic because it is being led by apostles that have been released by the Lord into the Body of Christ.

It is called a Reformation because it involves a re-design and re-structuring of the function and organization of the Church in the earth. The word Reformation is derived from the book of Hebrews and the pattern description of the vast spiritual and structural shift from the system of Law to the system of Grace as a *'diorthosis' (Gk)* or a Reformation or New Order.

Hebrews 9:10. NKJ
...concerned only with foods and drinks, various washings, and fleshly ordinances imposed until the time of reformation.

Hebrews 9:10 NIV
They are only a matter of food and drink and various ceremonial washings--external regulations applying until the time of the new order.

Some Definers of the Apostolic Reformation are:

- A total restructuring of the formation of the global church making obsolete the present shapes and emphases as God releases fresh revelation of His purposes and desires in the earth. One such change of formation is the movement from an emphasis on denominations to apostolic networks.

- A complete radical renovation of the mentality of the Church globally as God removes all aspects of limitation from our faith.

- A recognition that we are a generation of destiny that we are in the best position to actually bring an end to the ages in our time and arrive at the Finish of the purposes of God.

- A radical movement away from dead religious tradition and local church limitation to a Kingdom reality that invades every aspect of life. This is the rise of what is called 'Lifestyle Christianity'.

183

- A massive empowerment of ordinary believers and their emphatic movement to a place of full spiritual maturity and spiritual function thus radically broadening the base of the assault upon enemy positions in every area of life.

- A complete restructuring of the way the Kingdom is financed and the recognition and faith for huge financial input into the Kingdom for the push to the end of all things.

- A ferocious thrust into Governmental Prayer across the nations of the earth as a tidal wave of prayer and expectation from the people of God sweeps through the heavens and breaks satanic strongholds world-wide.

- A coordinated invasion of all territories internationally that have not yet received the declaration of the gospel of Jesus Christ.

- A deliberate, strategized, heightened warfare against illegitimate spiritual thrones in the heavens as God gives the Church insight and heightened powers of discernment.

- A purification of ministry and ministers as new leadership is shifted into place by the Lord, as a global reshuffling of leadership by the Lord is underway in the Church.

- The bringing back to effective recognition and operation of prophets and apostles to complete the function of the five governmental ministries of the Church.

- The achievement of a great momentum in the Church that will push it through to the ultimate end of all things.

- A final massive Evangelistic thrust and a global harvesting of the earth of souls for the Kingdom as God closes the ages down.

www.ingramcontent.com/pod-product-compliance
Lightning Source LLC
Chambersburg PA
CBHW071740120626
46550CB00002B/605